Conversations with Bernard Malamud

Literary Conversations Series

Peggy Whitman Prenshaw
General Editor

Conversations
with Bernard Malamud

Edited by
Lawrence M. Lasher

University Press of Mississippi
Jackson and London

Manufactured in the United States of America
94 93 92 91   4 3 2 1
The paper in this book meets the guidelines for permanence and
durability of the Committee on Production Guidelines for Book
Longevity of the Council on Library Resources.

Library of Congress Cataloging-in-Publication Data

Malamud, Bernard.
    Conversations with Bernard Malamud / edited by Lawrence Lasher.
      p. cm. — (Literary conversations series)
    Includes index.
    ISBN 0-87805-489-8 (alk. paper). — ISBN 0-87805-490-1 (pbk. :
alk. paper)
    1. Malamud, Bernard—Interviews. 2. Novelists, American—20th
century—Interviews. I. Lasher, Lawrence. II. Title.
III. Series.
PS3563.A4Z466   1991
  813′.54—dc20
                                         90-49374
                                           CIP

British Library Cataloging-in-Publication data available

Books by Bernard Malamud

The Natural. New York: Harcourt, Brace, 1952.
The Assistant. New York: Farrar, Straus & Cudahy, 1957.
The Magic Barrel. New York: Farrar, Straus & Cudahy, 1958.
A New Life. New York: Farrar, Straus & Giroux, 1961.
Idiots First. New York: Farrar, Straus & Giroux, 1963.
The Fixer. New York: Farrar, Straus & Giroux, 1966.
Pictures of Fidelman: An Exhibition. New York: Farrar, Straus & Giroux, 1969.
The Tenants. New York: Farrar, Straus & Giroux, 1971.
Rembrandt's Hat. New York: Farrar, Straus & Giroux, 1973.
Dubin's Lives. New York: Farrar, Straus & Giroux, 1979.
God's Grace. New York: Farrar, Straus & Giroux, 1982.
The Stories of Bernard Malamud. New York: Farrar Straus & Giroux, 1983.
The People and Uncollected Stories (unfinished novel and sixteen previously unpublished stories). Farrar, Straus & Giroux, 1989.

Contents

Introduction

Bernard Malamud's response to the last question in an interview conducted through the mail in 1973 is revealing of his general attitude toward interviews. Leslie and Joyce Field asked him if he could "think of other questions which have not been asked or which should be asked? Perhaps you can supply the answers for these unasked questions." Malamud's response was "No, I've talked too much." Only rarely a forthcoming subject for an interview, Malamud was faintly apologetic for his resistance to questions about his life and work and to the interview situation in general. In a cover note (15 July 1973) attached to his response to the Fields' written questions, he felt compelled to comment on the brevity of his answers: "I'm enclosing the questions and answers. I hope they're not too short or seemingly curt—I tend to speak to the point and avoid very much commentary." In a later note (8 August 1973) he said that his "reaction to your questions about my writing is par for the course. Please don't take it personally."[1]

Despite his discomfort with the interview situation, (Curt Suplee described his demeanor at the start of a *Washington Post* interview as that of a "brave man settling in for root canals") Malamud continued to give interviews throughout his writing career. His resistance to and impatience with interviews grew partly out of a Faulkner-like jealousy of his privacy. Many of the interviewers noted his general discomfort in talking about himself and he bluntly told one interviewer (Restivo), "I like my privacy." To another (Marshall) he noted that he found fame "inconvenient," because "it interferes with my privacy."

But beyond his temperamental desire for privacy, his dislike of interviews grew largely out of their potential to get between the

---

[1]References to items collected here appear in the text. Copies of both notes to the Fields are in the Malamud papers in the Library of Congress and are used with the permission of Mrs. Ann Malamud.

reader and the work. In the first interview in this collection (and very probably the first interview he gave) he asserted a point of view which, while he tempered it in later years, remained his essential attitude toward the potential distortions arising from a focus on the artist rather than the art. He told Joseph Wershba that "The work comes first. . . . The artist is secondary. There is much to be said for the old admonition, 'Never meet the artist.'" To Michiko Kakutani he observed that "there is too much interest in the teller, not the tale." An obsessive reviser, Malamud found the more or less spontaneous conversational format about his work intimidating and potentially misleading. Having gone through at least three laborious revisions of each book or story—"I love the flower of afterthought," he told Daniel Stern—he disliked making quick responses to large questions about the work. He preferred to have interviewers' questions submitted in advance and to have an opportunity to edit his responses. But that was rarely possible and one finds Malamud editing himself almost in mid-sentence. He interrupted Ralph Tyler with "Where I said I had become more flexible, could you change that to more relaxed?" Kakutani described him as speaking with "careful formality, emending his own statements for fluency and effect." He told the Fields (in their paraphrase) that he avoided interviews "'especially when tape recorders are relentlessly present' because he was often unhappy with his own responses."

But beyond his unease with the potential distortions of unedited language, Malamud believed strongly that once the writer let go of the work, it belonged to the reader and the writer had no business interfering with the dynamic and creative relationship between the reader and the text. Although his pedagogical instincts did, on occasion, seduce him into more or less extended speculation on the meaning of a text, he saw such authorial pronouncement as a disservice to the work and to the reader. This reservation comes clear in the Fields' introduction to their interview with him: He "disliked explaining his fiction because by describing his 'intent' he may in effect 'betray' his work. He fears that people may substitute what he says about his writing for their own imaginative reading of his fiction. Thus a certain kind of interview could be self-defeating." Some thirteen years and over a score of interviews later, Malamud expressed essentially the same reservation when he interrupted his response to a question about the meaning of *God's Grace* with "You know one thing that I don't like about what we're doing is that I have begun to explain my fiction, and I don't like to do that. . . . For years I have avoided answering questions of this kind." A few moments later, the interviewer, Joel Salzberg, (1986) asked "Why are you still giving interviews . . .? It seems that both now and in the past you have been torn between a desire to discuss your work and a need to remain private. Have you been able to balance the two?" Malamud's response revealed his essential ambivalence about interviews: "Not always successfully. There is in me a certain kindness. I like to be of assistance if I can do it in a way that doesn't threaten me as an artist. . . ."

The writer's desire "to be of assistance" kept him making himself available to interviewers and doing his best to overcome his instinctive and principled resistance. As late as 1979 Malamud was still working at making himself more accessible. When Ralph Tyler noted that he was known to "be reluctant about interviews," Malamud indicated that this reluctance was "a thing of the past" when he "hadn't really organized [himself] for interviews. Now I can handle them with greater ease."

On the right occasion and in the hands of a sympathetic inter- viewer who knew the work well and was more likely to ask "writerly" questions, Malamud was likely to be more expansive and responsive than was his habit in the typical journalist or academic-to-writer format where he "was often disappointed by people talking to me about work they hadn't bothered to read" (Field and Field). Curt Leviant, an interviewer and a novelist, told the editor in response to a comment on the unusual quality of the responses he had elicited from the writer, "I'm sure it was not my skill or talent in the M[alamud] interview; we just hit it off and he shmoozed at length."

The settings of the interviews, as well as the impressions of the man interviewers went away with, reflect something of this same double- ness. They range from more or less clipped responses to written or telephoned questions, to a relaxed lunch on the porch of the house in Bennington, Vermont, or through several sessions during a week- end birthday celebration. The prevailing impression of the writer rests somewhere between a somewhat chilling formality—recurrent lan- guage includes "disciplined" and "austere"—one describes him as "solemn and professorial"—and a "quietly gracious" warmth and simplicity. If he is "outward going" (Hughes), he is also "resolutely austere" (Kakutani).

Whatever the inherent limitations of the form and Malamud's sometimes reluctant participation, the interviews are the chief source of information about the writer's vision of his world and his work since he left little prose outside of the fiction and no significant collection of letters has yet surfaced. The interviews are a rich source of authorial commentary on a wide range of topics and are invaluable in providing a limited but often sharply outlined picture of the man behind the books.

Malamud was always resistant to readings of his books which made reductive, one-to-one connections between him and characters in his fiction. "Without invention," Malamud told one interviewer, "biographical details remain merely strings of uncooked spaghetti,"[2] and he argued for a more complex relationship between character and author, "autobiographical essence rather than autobiographical history" (Stern). But questions about his life are present in almost every interview and Malamud answered them patiently. The interviews offer a sketchy but sometimes revealing account of his early years with emphasis on his youthful impulse to story-telling, early encouragement from teachers, and the influence of the movies and boy's books. He spoke often of the formative influence of a childhood world—the world of Jewish immigrants—which focussed on the "welfare of human beings . . . what makes a man function as a man."[3] The interviews offer glimpses of the writer's education from the beginning through his M.A. at Columbia in 1942 and record the search for work in a depressed New York City between 1936 and 1940 when he began teaching high school. But the recurrent theme is always the writing, and the picture of Malamud one takes from these sketches is of a very serious young man struggling to stay alive as a writer when the writer has not yet been born.

There is little biographical material after his move to Oregon in 1949 and his subsequent experience in Vermont. His responses to questions about the academic life in Corvallis and Bennington were

[2]Anatole Broyard, "Being a Character," New York Times Book Review, 22 November 1981, p. 55.

[3]Thomas Lask, "Malamud's Lives," New York Times Book Review, 21 January 1979, p. 43.

invariably positive, but his academic career was always distinctly secondary to the writing. The emphasis remained focussed on the discipline of the writing life, on "the life of the imagination" and "the privileges of form" (Stern).

Interviewers were almost inevitably interested in the forms which the enactment of that "life of the imagination" took. Questions about the requisites for the writing life are frequent. First, there must be talent and, secondly, the writer must discover his subject matter— what he has to say. But these would not suffice, Malamud said again and again, without discipline. The writing act, he said in several contexts, is a moral act, an enactment of that struggle with the self which is a fundamental theme of many of his fictions. As he told Leah Garchick, "the secret to becoming a good writer lies in the self, in self-study, discipline, maturity; in constantly seeking the highest opportunities to do well." Always the emphasis was on the demands of the work and the self-sacrifice implied by a commitment to art. When Malamud was asked to give advice to young writers, the message was "getting organized to use your talents" (Long), "getting into your small room, sitting at the table, excluding many of the pleasures of the world, and very seriously writing and writing, doing the burden of the work that has to be done" (Pollit). Anything which interfered with the writing was to be resisted. The reader of the interviews will note, for instance, that Malamud was ambivalent about teaching and that the ambivalence arose from its demands on his time. On balance, despite its interference with the writing, "teaching helps more than it hinders" since it keeps the writer "in touch with people" (Field and Field), and by providing a living allows a writer to "maintain his freedom" (Pollit). Further, he said, "a community of serious readers is a miraculous thing" (Stern). Still, to the extent that the academic world is a shelter from the fully-lived life, Malamud, "in the best of all possible worlds," would not recommend it. He told Curt Suplee that he'd "advise a writer to live his life as fully as he can, and then write about it."

During his teaching career, Malamud taught both creative writing and literature courses and indicated that he almost never taught his own works in the latter since an "author cannot dictate the total meaning of his work to a classroom" (Frankel). He was consistently reluctant in the interviews as well—especially in the earlier inter-

views—to "explain his fiction." He valued "imaginative interpretations . . . whether I agree with them or not" (Leviant). He refused
to answer a question about mythology in *The Assistant* with "You
read the book and write your own ticket" (Stern). In another place in
the same interview he addressed the reader: "You can read?—all
right, tell me what my books mean. Astonish me." He rejected the
notion that there was a correct interpretation of his work. He hoped
not (Field and Field). Each reader, he said, "brings to a novel the
pattern of his own life, and so he reads it in a slightly different way"
(Pollit).

If Malamud resisted talking about the meaning of individual works,
several of the interviewers were successful in drawing him out on the
more general question of themes in his fictions. Always insisting on
the necessity to embody theme in "significant form" and wary of the
danger of the overly-didactic, Malamud was seduced not infrequently
into attempting to define his thematic preoccupations at the broadest
level of abstraction. While the various formulations differ widely in
tone and focus, they are all, finally, centered in Malamud's large and
comprehensive moral vision which, he seems to say, arises out of the
paradoxical struggle to win freedom for the self through a victory
over the self. His characters "are engaged in the enterprise" to
"transcend the self—to extend one's realm of freedom" (Stern). He is
interested in man's "best efforts to produce a greater freedom than
he was born with" (Benedict). He alluded to this fundamental
"commitment to the human"—the idea of extending one's own
freedom and thereby the freedom of others—as it arose in many
different fictional contexts, e.g., sexuality and love, the commitment
to art, the metaphor of prison and the centrality of the notion of
suffering. He spoke of the "strong theme" of "self-understanding in
the work, since if one is to win the battle with the self, one must
"penetrate the mystery of the self" (Suplee).

The notion of the "commitment to the human" as a major theme
of his work got additional expression in the interviews when Malamud
was questioned about the nature of the relationship of the artist to
society. Malamud had much to say in several of the interviews about
the artist's social and political responsibility. For instance, in a late
interview (1983) focussed on the just-published *God's Grace*, he
suggested a direct social responsibility for the writer when he said

that he had "a sense now . . . of peril. . . . I feel it is the writer's business to cry havoc, because silence can't increase understanding or evoke mercy" (Benedict). He not infrequently connected specific political and social events with his fiction, acknowledging the source of his moral vision in the larger events of the twentieth century. He cited most often as formative influences on his fiction, World War II and the Holocaust, the racial strife of the sixties and early seventies, and the nuclear threat of the cold war.

Questions about the sources and content of Malamud's work almost inevitably touched upon his Jewishness as a writer and as a man. Malamud always resisted the notion of the "Jewish writer." The burden of his answers to questions about Jewish-American writers was that the term was "schematic and reductive" (Field and Field): "I write about Jews because I know them. I'm comfortable with them" (Leviant). Beyond his knowledge of Jews, however, he acknowledged that the connection between himself and the Jewish experience was a complex one. Malamud explained that he wrote about Jews not only because he knew them well, but "because they set my imagination going" (Stern). What is implicit in the fiction is clearly stated and elaborated in several of the longer interviews. The Jew in Malamud's fiction functions metaphorically, for Jewish history is a "metaphor for the fate of all men" (Leviant). Malamud's elaboration of this point will bring the reader close to the bone of his central moral vision since in his reiterated attempts to define what it is in the Jewish experience that attracted him, Malamud is drawn again and again to language about "the struggle against self" (Leviant) as the core of the Jewish ethical experience.

Malamud's resistance to the provincialism implied by the "Jewish-writer" label—"I write for Indians, Japanese, Hungarians, British—any one who can read" (Masilamoni)—is a prominent element of his responses to questions about literary influence as well. While he acknowledged his reading in Jewish literature, he made clear that the major influences on him were American and, to a lesser extent, European. He told Curt Suplee that his "whole history as a writer is in connection much more with American literature than with any other kind," and in at least two of the interviews he read approvingly from critical essays which connect him with James and Hawthorne.

If Malamud read criticism, he didn't write it. Aside from an essay

adapted from his 1967 National Book Award acceptance speech[4]
and his introductory essay to *Stories* (Farrar, Straus & Giroux, 1983)
the interviews contain what we have of Malamudian theory and
criticism. The central argument of the New York *Times* essay resists
what Malamud took to be the "mindlessness" of the "new novel"
practiced by "some who want fiction refined almost to pure form."
The interviews reflect that same resistance to what Malamud saw as
the excesses of the modernist and post-modernist program. If
Malamud took pride in being what he described in many of the
interviews as an imaginative writer who was willing to experiment
and to take chances, he insisted finally, on the centrality of story and
theme and of the role of literature as a commentary on human
experience. The issue comes up obliquely in several of the interviews,
perhaps most clearly in the interview with Israel Shenker in which
Malamud insisted on the importance of "story" as the "basic element
of fiction—though that idea is not popular with disciples of the 'new
novel.'" Malamud went on to make the all-important connection
between story-telling and the fundamental affirmation of human
possibilities, for it is in story-telling that we discover and affirm our
humanity: "The story will be with us as long as man is. You know
that in part because of its effect on children. It's through story they
realize that mystery won't kill them. Through story they learn they
have a future."

On more narrow critical questions, Malamud did not have a great
deal to say in the interviews. He commented interestingly in several
places on the independence of his characters whom he "can't outguess all the time although God knows I try" (Suplee). He described
his characters as taking on a life of their own, "begin[ning] to run,
take off, and then you're surprised at the qualities and speed they
pick up."

For all the somber tones of Malamud's fiction, his readers and his
critics understand the central role of comedy in his work, and in the
interviews he commented frequently and interestingly on humor as
an element of his fiction. While he avoided responding to reductive
questions about whether his vision was tragic or comic, he was quick
to affirm the central place of the comic in his work, both as a neces-

[4]"Speaking of Books: Theme, Content and the 'New Novel,'" *New York Times Book Review*, 26 March 1967, p. 2, 29.

sary resistance to despair—"to live sanely one must discover—or invent it" (Field and Field)—and as a kind of a prod to imagination and invention—"With me humor comes unexpectedly. . . . When something starts funny I can feel my imagination eating and running" (Stern). He told Daniel Stern (and others) that Chaplin was a major influence on him, and he defined an aesthetic of humor which readers will recognize from the short stories when he describes Chaplin's effect as " . . . the rhythm, the snap of comedy; the reserved comic presence—that beautiful distancing; the funny with the sad; the surprise of surprise."

Malamud was frequently asked questions about the short story as a form, and he commented interestingly on the story as a kind of refuge from the novel which "takes a lot out of you" (Heller). Writing stories, he told Daniel Stern, allowed him "to breathe" between novels and gave him "time to think what's in the next book." If, in the introduction to *Stories* Malamud had emphasized the brevity of the story form as its primary attraction ("The payoff is faster. The effect may be startlingly right."), almost twenty years earlier he made essentially the same point to Granville Hicks when he said that the challenge of the story is "to say everything that must be said and to say it quickly, fleetingly, as though two people had met for a moment in a restaurant, or a railroad station, and one had time only to tell the other that they are both human, and here, this story proves it." In the *Paris Review* interview he described the short story as "packing a self or two into a few pages, predicating lifetimes," a description he would repeat almost verbatim some ten years later in the introductory essay to *Stories*.

Since the occasion for many of the interviews was the publication of a new novel, there was a certain amount of conversation about the individual books, though much of it is repetitious and limited by the writer's resistance to saying much about the individual work. In discussions of *The Natural*, the emphasis was on the sources of the book in his childhood in Brooklyn and in his reading in Joyce, Mann, and Eliot. Discussions of *The Assistant* identified its sources in his childhood experience of his father's grocery store and in three early short stories. He talked about the book being in the European tradition and continuing his examination of the notion of the heroic as he had begun it in *The Natural*. An interesting comment on the impulse to the novel is his recollection that after *The Natural* he "wanted to do a more serious, deeper, perhaps more realistic piece of work" (Hicks).

The conversations about *A New Life,* Malamud's "academic novel," included his frequently reiterated rejection of attempts to identify him with Sy Levin, the protagonist-professor whose adventures in Cascadia tempted interviewers to draw overly-literal parallels with Bernard Malamud in Corvallis. Malamud rejected the one-to-one connection and said that the novel was a continuation of the apprentice theme as he had developed it in *The Assistant.* As was his almost invariable habit in talking about a new book, he emphasized the ways in which the book departed from earlier work. He told Joseph Wershba while the book was in progress, that "It's different from anything I've done. . . . It'll be something new for my readers, and the first time for me: a romantic love story, with warmth and richness."

Although interviewers wanted to talk about the humanistic themes of *The Fixer,* Malamud was at pains to talk about the book as a narrative experiment and a new departure for him. The challenge, he said, in several places, was to disinvent history and create myth. The interviews which focus on *The Fixer* are interesting as well for the emphasis they place on Malamud's decision to address himself to contemporary political concerns. He spoke eloquently in several of the interviews of the interaction between his research into an historical event and his concern with contemporary instances of injustice.

The few comments on *Pictures of Fidelman* emphasized the experimental form of the book and its comic quality. Discussion of *The Tenants* focussed on its genesis in the racial strife in New York in the sixties and the rise of black activism, as well as Malamud's strong reservations about what he took to be the politicization of literature in the then-new "black aesthetic."

Dubin's Lives, his seventh novel, was he said, a reversion to nineteenth-century forms reflecting his admiration for Hardy and George Eliot. *Dubin,* he said, was intended as a "big" novel. It was to be no minimalist or post-modernist exercise like "some fiction I read, [in which] the author doesn't really show what else he's got; he gets into a kind of Samuel Beckett mode and sings one tune forever" (Pollit).

Surprisingly, given Malamud's stature as a master of the short form, there is little commentary on individual stories or collections of stories in the interviews.

The interviews collected here present a necessarily fragmented but valuable and interesting picture of Malamud as a man and as an artist. Aside from his seriousness of purpose and the almost awesome self-discipline which transformed that purpose into enduring work, the two sides of Bernard Malamud which emerge most clearly from the interviews are the adventurous, experimental artist who took pride in himself as a "daring writer," and the moralist and teacher who frequently quoted Camus': "The purpose of the writer is to keep civilization from destroying itself."

The restless search for new and effective form was a constant in Malamud's work and gets its best expression in his response to Joel Salzberg's attempt to get him to say something about *The People,* the novel he was working on when he died in 1986. Only months before his death and after a debilitating stroke the writer was still "reinventing" himself. Salzberg asked him if the novel represented a new direction in his work:

No question about it. It's one of the things that has me on tenterhooks about whether I can make it come off. . . . I am reminded of a question that someone asked Matisse about the transformation that took place from his earliest to his latest work. He replied that he felt anxiety every time he was trying to paint something new and later astonishment after seeing his work successfully completed. Whenever he felt that anxiety, he had to reinvent himself into existence by taking chances he had never taken before.

Malamud as moralist is visible throughout the fiction and is present in virtually all these "conversations." The daring writer who reinvented himself with each book wrote always with Camus' formulation in mind, and, despite the dark vision—the stories about characters who "opened doors like corpses adjusting their own coffin lids" (Wershba)—Malamud's vision never wavered from his description of it in the first interview in this collection: "My premise is for humanism—and against nihilism. And that is what I try to put in my writing" (Wershba). It is out of the marriage of that premise—"a kind of experimental optimism"—to the discipline and daring of the artist, that the sad and wonderful stories of Bernard Malamud were born.

As with other books in the Literary Conversations series, the interviews are reprinted uncut and unedited except for the silent correction of obvious errors and the regularization of titles of books into italics. In a collection such as this there is bound to be a certain amount of repetition. Inevitably, interviewers asked the same questions and often got similar, even identical, responses. On the other hand, every interview selected for inclusion adds something to the portrait of Malamud which finally emerges.

I would like to acknowledge the help of the Graduate School of the University of Maryland at Baltimore for providing financial support for this project. I am indebted to the fine professional staff of the University of Maryland Baltimore County library, particularly to Chuck D'Adamo who tracked down many of the more elusive items included here. I would also like to acknowledge the assistance of Professor Slo Petrovich of the UMBC psychology department who gave generously of his time and his knowledge of Serbo-Croation in helping me to understand the content of an article which, ultimately, was not included in the collection. Professor Joel Salzberg of the University of Colorado and Professor Robert Solotaroff of the University of Minnesota were quick to respond to inquiries and Professor Salzberg was kind enough to permit me to include his previously unpublished 1983 interview with Malamud. Janet Goetz and Susan Harrell were helpful in a hundred ways, most particularly in turning incomprehensible notes and odd pieces of paper into respectable correspondence and ordered files. I also wish to thank Mrs. Malamud for her permission to quote from her husband's two notes to the Fields; she also granted permission to reprint material which late editorial decisions removed from the collection.

Finally, I thank my wife, Reva, for the many forms of her support, most notably, her graceful yielding of her dining room table to my files of photocopies and correspondence for the last several months.

LML
August 1990

Chronology

1914 Born 26 April, Brooklyn, New York, to Russian immigrants, Max and Bertha Fidelman Malamud

1928–32 Attends Erasmus Hall High School, Brooklyn

1929 Mother dies

1932–36 Attends City College; B.A. 1936.

1936–40 Works at a variety of temporary factory and sales jobs; does graduate work at Columbia; takes teacher training and civil service examinations; tutors immigrants in English; works at the Census Bureau in Washington, D.C.

1940–48 Teaches evening high school classes at Erasmus Hall High School; works on a completed but unpublished novel, "The Light Sleeper."

1942 M.A. from Columbia University, thesis on Thomas Hardy's *The Dynasts*

1943 First story publications in *Threshold* and *American Preface*

1945 Marries Ann de Chiara and moves to Greenwich Village

1947 Son, Paul, is born.

1948–49 Teaches high school evening classes in Harlem

1949–61   Teaches at Oregon State College (now Oregon State
          University) at Corvallis

1950   First commercial publication; stories in *Partisan Review,
          Harper's Bazaar* and *Commentary.*

1952   *The Natural*; birth of daughter, Janna.

1956–57   *Partisan Review*–Rockefeller Grant and sabbatical leave
          for travel in Europe, residence in Rome

1957   *The Assistant*

1958   Short story collection, *The Magic Barrel;* the Rosenthal
          Foundation Award of the National Institute of Arts and
          Letters and the Daroff Memorial Award for *The Assistant.*

1959   The National Book Award for *The Magic Barrel* and a
          Ford Foundation Fellowship

1961   *A New Life*; joins the faculty of language and literature at
          Bennington College, Bennington, Vermont.

1963   Short story collection, *Idiot's First;* travels in England and
          Italy.

1964   Elected to the American Academy, National Institute of
          Arts and Letters

1965   Travels in Spain, France, and the Soviet Union

1966   *The Fixer*

1966–68   Visiting lecturer at Harvard

1967   National Book Award and Pulitzer Prize for *The Fixer;*
          elected to the American Academy of Arts and Sciences.

1968   Visits Israel

1969   *Pictures of Fidelman: An Exhibition*

1971   *The Tenants*

1973   Short story collection, *Rembrandt's Hat*

1976   Jewish Heritage Award

1979   Governor's Award, Vermont Council on the Arts. *Dubin's Lives.*

1979–81   President of P.E.N.

1980   Member, American Academy–Institute of Arts and Letters

1981   Brandeis Creative Arts Award

1981–82   Fellow of the Center for Advanced Study in the Behaviorial Sciences, Palo Alto, California

1982   *God's Grace;* heart surgery and subsequent stroke.

1983   *The Stories of Bernard Malamud;* the American Academy– Institute Gold Medal for Fiction.

1986   Dies 18 March

Conversations with Bernard Malamud

Not Horror but Sadness

Joseph Wershba/1958

From *The New York Post,* 14 September, 1958. Reprinted by permission of The New York Post Co., Inc.

America's least known writer of the first rank was in town the other day.

He is Bernard Malamud, author of *The Assistant* and *The Magic Barrel,* and a man who thinks too much fuss is made over writers anyway.

"The work comes first," he says. "The artist is secondary. There is much to be said for the old admonition, 'Never meet the artist.'"

At 44, Malamud is a youthful man. He was born in Brooklyn, educated in New York schools and is now an assistant professor of English at an Oregon college. He is gentle, soft-spoken and completely disciplined in thought and speech.

He has written primarily about Jews and their sorrows, but in a manner hitherto unknown in American literature.

"I write about Jews because I know them. But more important, I write about them because the Jews are absolutely the very *stuff* of drama."

Malamud is consumed with the drama of personality fulfilling itself. This should be the chief business of the writer, he says.

"The sell-out of personality is just tremendous. Our most important natural resource is Man. The times cry out for men of imagination and hope. Instead, our fiction is loaded with sickness, homosexuality, fragmented man, 'other-directed' man. It should be filled with love and beauty and hope. We are underselling Man. And American fiction is at its weakest when we go in for journalistic case studies instead of rich personality development."

A group of influential critics on the smaller quarterlies has already raised Malamud to the top echelon of American writers today.

Norman Podhoretz, a leading voice among the younger critics, says that Malamud's work "seems a kind of miracle, an act of spiritual

3

autonomy perfect enough to persuade us that the possibility of freedom from the determinings of history and sociology still exist."

Harvey Swados feels Malamud is "one writer in a thousand," and that "from now on, anyone who pretends to speak seriously, either here or abroad, of the American literary scene will have to come to grips with his vision of the inner reality of American life.

Herbert Gold, in the *Nation,* called Malamud's writings "lyric marvels—the headlong architectural daring of a great novelist." Leslie Fiedler talks of Malamud's "poetry," and adds: "It is odd how the subdued tone, the show of 'realism' takes us in, as life itself takes us in, with its routine surfaces."

To Meyer Levin, Malamud "certainly counts amongst the literary figures of our day." New York Times critic Charles Poore notes that the Malamud stories "have a wide range, but what is most memorable about them is their depth."

For the most part, however, Malamud is an "artistic success"— which means that he suffers the usual penalty of that breed by not having the great audiences which Whitman said great writers require. Malamud's work has already been compared favorably to the mainstream of Flaubert, Dostoyevsky, Tolstoy and Sherwood Anderson.

The Assistant, he says, "is in the European tradition. So am I." But he adds quickly with a smile, "My next book will be an 'American' novel. It's different from anything I've done. I've just finished a chapter working on it up at Yaddo (the upstate writer's colony) and it's beginning to open for me. It'll be something new for my readers, and the first time for me: a romantic love story, with warmth and richness."

"It's the story of a New Yorker who goes out West to begin a new spiritual life. No, it's not autobiographical. It is about a teacher who is Jewish, but he will be operating in a non-Jewish milieu."

Malamud's writings have stirred discussion and controversy as have those of few other writers this past decade. Malamud cares about his characters—and so do his readers.

"There is too much gloom and doom, too much horror," some have told him, in his writing.

"Not horror," he replies softly. "Sadness." And with that one word comes an understanding of Malamud's 'European' approach—the rich, story-telling approach, tragedy piled on tragedy, the absence of self-pity or bathos by the author.

Frank Alpine, the Italian, "Assistant," watches the funeral of his Jewish benefactor and thinks: "Suffering is like a piece of goods. I bet the Jews could make a suit of clothes out of it. The other funny thing is that there are more of them around than anybody knows."

It develops that "there *are* more of them around," for Frank becomes a Jew and the problem of "Jewish suffering" becomes really a problem of "humanity's suffering."

The novel, as well as most of the short stories in *The Magic Barrel,* reflects the drama which Malamud sees in the history of the Jews: "First, the Prophets' 'way of gentleness;' the Sins of the People, Punishment, Exile and Return." This, he says, makes one of the most dramatic canvases of all time: "It is the primal problem of man seeking to escape the tragedy of the past."

Of course, the most impossible situation in the world is debating an author on the meaning of his works. Malamud recalls with pain the well-intentioned lady in Boston who said of the *macher* in *The Assistant*—the arsonist—"it was a shame to have put him in."

"The writers job," he says, "is to create the architecture, the form and the content. Once he does that, his job is done. The artist cannot legislate the reader's interpretation. Nor can the artist give the *complete* interpretation. Otherwise, there'd be nothing to write about. Life is not totally comprehensible. Imagination is required."

But Malamud fights hard for what he believes to be valid interpretations of his works.

Making Frank Alpine in *The Assistant* an Italian was a careful calculation. "Italians and Jews are closely related in their consciousness of the importance of personality," Malamud says, "in their emphasis on the richness of life, in their tremendous sense of past and tradition."

Only once during the interview did Malamud become edgy with emotion. That was when he said:

"The suffering of the Jews is a distinct thing for me. I for one believe that not enough has been made of the tragedy of the destruction of 6,000,000 Jews.

"And I felt exactly the same in 1936 when the Yellow River flooded and six to ten million Chinese were drowned. Not enough has been made of such tragedies.

"Somebody has to cry—even if it's just a writer, 20 years later."

Malamud's writings have no "politics," and yet they are drenched in two political waves. Implicit in much of the writing is the politics of barbarism—the backdrop of Hitlerism and its victims and, secondly, the Great Depression.

Bernard Malamud went to PS 181, Erasmus Hall High, CCNY uptown and Columbia.

"I was discovered at 16," he grins. "My compositions received high grades and my work appeared in the high school magazine. People sometimes don't understand how utterly essential it is for students to have their worth recognized by their teachers.

"I remember in college, Prof. Earl Fenton Palmer wrote on my paper: 'This work reminds me of two other of my students: Lewis Mumford and Irwin Edman.' I couldn't walk home that night. I was up in the air. The reward, the richness, the revelation of that comment by Prof. Palmer has never been duplicated.

"And then there was Prof. Theodore Goodman. He taught me to beware of being dishonest as a writer. He said to me: 'Either you go in honest or you sink.' And I've tried to stick to that ever since.

"So you sit down, years later, in a rooming house in Brooklyn, and you write, write, write and write, until something comes forth that shows promise—and not until then can you even begin to think of yourself as a writer."

For a while, he taught night school for adults at Erasmus. In 1949, living in Greenwich Village, married and with a 2 year-old son, Malamud searched for the answer to a very precise problem:

"How can I make a living—and still write?"

There were three college teaching offers. He accepted the one from Oregon State College, at Corvallis. The pay was $3500. It has since improved. He is now assistant professor of English. He gives courses in composition, creative writing and literature.

He set himself a strict regimen to which he has adhered for nine years. Half his time is spent teaching, the other half writing. Mondays, Wednesdays and Fridays are for classes, office hours, paper grading. Tuesdays, Thursdays, Saturdays ("and I sneak parts of Sundays") are for his novels and short stories.

In the past nine years he has turned out two novels—*The Natural*, an allegorical baseball story, and *The Assistant*—and *The Magic*

Barrel, a short story collection. *The Assistant* was based on two of his short stories. It has won a number of awards, including the Rosenthal Award of the National Institute of Arts and Letters. In 1956 he won a Partisan Review fellowship for a year in Italy with his wife Ann, his son Paul and his daughter Janna, now 7.

Malamud has not made a living at writing. "The books have paid for car repairs, an encyclopedia set for the children, maybe a washing machine," he says. "We live on our income from the college." He'd like to devote more time to writing.

Asked about "influences," he begins to enumerate, then gives up. In the short story, he has deep debts to Anderson, Hemingway, Joyce, Chekhov and Katherine Mansfield. In the novel, his influences are the Bible, Shakespeare, Dostoyevsky, Tolstoy, Flaubert, Hardy, Hemingway and Faulkner.

"And in the new book—Stendahl."

He has also been influenced by painters. "Remember what Hemingway has said, how painting teaches us to write? Painters, of necessity, have to abstract, they have to highlight, they have to compress."

Malamud spent last month writing full-time at Yaddo, and came into town to see his publishers, Farrar, Straus & Cudahy. He is also checking developments in the possible stage adaptation of *The Assistant.*

"The purpose of the writer," says Malamud, "is to keep civilization from destroying itself. But without preachment. Artists, cannot be ministers. As soon as they attempt it, they destroy their artistry."

Malamud, whose characters have at times "opened doors, like corpses adjusting their own coffin lids," nevertheless lives with hope:

"My premise is that we will not destroy each other. My premise is that we will live on. We will seek a better life. We may not become better, but at least we will seek betterment.

"My premise," says Bernard Malamud, "is for humanism—and against nihilism. And that is what I try to put in my writings."

Author Finds Room to Breathe in Corvallis

Jack Rosenthal/1959

From *The Oregonian* (Portland) 12 April 1959, Copyright ©
1959 by The Oregonian Publishing Co. Reprinted by permission.

A woman at a party recently asked Bernard Malamud, "How do you
live in Corvallis?" "I breathe," replied the 44-year-old Oregon State
College English instructor, who has just won the National Book
Award for the outstanding work of fiction in 1959.

There was as much truth as irony in his reply. Malamud wasn't
simply parrying a thrust at a lack of culture in Oregon. When he
writes, he is a man in a box—nailed tight with discipline. When he
comes out, there is a need to breathe.

In Corvallis, he has been able to. He moved there 10 years ago
from New York, where "the sheer technology of living had become
too complicated. I needed a little light, a little air, a little space to
think."

He talked quickly and confidently in his neat, book-lined living
room. "There's a certain substantial sweetness and honesty and
wholesomeness in the people around us here. And I like Corvallis
because I enjoy spending a good deal of time with my family. I
delight in walking to school and walking home for lunch."

But even those pleasures are limited by his greatest one, writing.
When he is engrossed in a book, he gives up even the walks home
for lunch.

"His wife brings a sack lunch to his office," relates an OSC
colleague, Faith Norris. "Sometimes, she doesn't even go inside. She
just taps on the window and hands it to him."

His remarkable discipline has had remarkable results. He has
written two published novels, *The Natural*, about a 34-year-old
baseball rookie, published in 1952, and *The Assistant,* about a Jewish
storekeeper in New York, which last year won a Rosenthal award of
the National Institute of Arts and Letters.

He also has written a number of short stories and it was a

collection of some of these, *The Magic Barrel,* which last month won for him the coveted National Book Award.

The title story won the Partisan Review fellowship, which he used to go to Rome, and recently he was one of 11 American writers chosen for a creative arts grant from the Ford Foundation.

He is on that grant now, freed from teaching for two years, and is working on a third novel.

All of the fruits of Malamud's work have come in Oregon; until he moved here he hadn't even sold a story. But the groundwork was already laid—stretching back to 1922 and the third grade.

He always wanted to be a writer after that. At Erasmus Hall High School in Brooklyn, he won a medal for an essay, which, like *The Assistant,* was based on his youth in his father's grocery store.

He continued to write at City College of New York and at Columbia, where he earned his master's degree—and then went to work. But, "I never took seriously some of the miserable jobs I had. I always wanted to be a writer."

One valuable experience he recalls was tutoring German refugees in English. "They were an education to me. I learned whole new areas of art and literature from them. They were educated people of all sorts."

One of his pupils was an actor, who later appeared in a movie. "I went to see it, with great anticipation to find out how good a tutoring job I had done. He didn't say a word. He was in most of the movie, but his part was all pantomime."

Finally, in 1940, he got an evening job at his old high school, which left his days free to write, and he did.

The next 10 years were important ones. He didn't sell a story, but he learned. It was a time spent "learning what I could write about" and developing what he describes as "an idea of life, of values. You need a view of life to be a writer. You need to see yourself in a historical perspective."

And it was a time for reading. "A writer must read an enormous amount. If he does not, he's thin. He has no idea what the universe means. You have to develop a sense of spirit."

Perhaps as important is a sense of discipline. "Discipline is an ideal for the self. If you have to discipline yourself to achieve art, you discipline yourself. If you have to sit in an office constantly for six days a week to write, you do it, and you become a writer."

This discipline extends beyond his writing and has won him the respect of his colleagues at Oregon State.

"Bernie is one of the most efficient people I've ever been on a committee with," says Mrs. Norris. "If anyone wanders off the subject, he has a knack of getting things right back on the track."

The discipline also affects his family. "When he's writing," says his attractive wife, with warmth, "he's alone. Whether we're in Rome or New York or Corvallis, he's alone."

His wife and two children, Paul, 11, and Janna, 7, are understanding. Just before Malamud returned from a trip last year, Paul teased: "When daddy comes back, the feudal system will be in effect again."

Malamud is a devoted father. His associates tell of the hours he spends playing games with his children or reading to them. Indeed, a warmth and simplicity penetrate even the veneer he displays in an interview.

When he saw a picture and feature story done about him in New York, he was proud, but not because of the plaudits it contained. "Ann, Ann," he called quickly to his wife. "Look at this picture. It shows me in my new suit!"

His Hopes on the Human Heart

Granville Hicks/1963

From *Saturday Review,* 12 October 1963, 31-32. Reprinted by
Permission of Omni Publications International Ltd.

Bernard Malamud was born in Brooklyn in 1914, of parents who
came from Russia though they had met in this country. After a short
time in the butter and egg business, driving a horse and wagon, his
father bought a small grocery store. Since his mother helped in the
store, which stayed open until late, Malamud had little family life and
grew up as something of a street kid. At the same time he liked
school, and at an early age was encouraged to write. He attended
Erasmus Hall High School, was a better than average student, and
took a strong interest in the *Erasmian,* the school magazine, of which
he became an editor. He wrote many stories for the magazine, and
he also took part in dramatics.

He entered the City College of New York in 1932, at the bottom of
the Depression, and his years there were not very happy. He liked
the college well enough, but three hours a day on the subway was an
ordeal. Unlike many of his contemporaries, he never became interested in radical causes. He had his own problems, and he distrusted
the Communists, especially after the Moscow trials.

After graduation he had a series of jobs, in a factory, in a store, and
as a clerk in the Census Bureau in Washington, but he wanted to
write, and a teaching position seemed likeliest to give him an opportunity. In 1940 he began to teach night classes at Erasmus Hall High
School and continued to do so until 1948. In 1949 he taught night
classes in Harlem. Meanwhile he had taken his master's degree at
Columbia and had married Ann de Chiara.

During the Forties he wrote constantly—among other things a
novel that he destroyed. Several of his stories were published in non-
commercial magazines, but it was not until 1949 that he was paid for
a story, "The Cost of Living," which appeared in *Harper's Bazaar*
and is included in his latest volume, *Idiots First.* Although he has his
doubts about "influences," he had read a good deal in the work of

11

the Russians—Dostoevsky, Gogol, and Chekhov—whom he found
congenial. He was also interested in Joyce and Mann, and was
attracted to the short short stories of Sherwood Anderson and Ernest
Hemingway. He read some Jewish literature—Sholem Aleichem and
I.L. Peretz—in translation, and later became acquainted with I. B.
Singer's works.

By 1947, after their first child was born, he and his wife were
increasingly eager to get out of the city, and in the summer of 1949
he accepted an offer from Oregon State College, where for a dozen
years he taught composition and literature. Although there were
certain aspects of state college life that he did not admire, as he was
to make clear in *A New Life,* he was not dissatisfied with his position;
his first four books were all written while he was on the staff of the
college.

His first published novel was *The Natural* (1952), a treatment of
baseball in terms of myth. He had been reading Joyce and Mann and
Eliot, and he was also impressed by Jessie L. Weston's *From Ritual to
Romance,* which provided the mythic matter of Eliot's *The Waste
Land.* He was not so much interested in baseball for itself as in the
American hero. He was asking himself why a man of great talents
should sell out in America, and he saw in his material opportunity for
comic effects as well as for a drama of moral issues. (Comedy, he
believes, is really more difficult to write than tragedy, and he holds
that the more of it a writer can get into his fiction, the more imaginative his work tends to be.) Although it puzzled some readers, *The
Natural* has its strong admirers. Leslie Fiedler writes in *Love and
Death in the American Novel* that *The Natural* "was largely ignored,
perhaps because the lively play of fantasy, the trifling with illusion
which characterize it disconcerted those who had picked it up
expecting a 'good baseball yarn.'" "Actually," he continues, "it *is* a
baseball story, disconcertingly out of Ring Lardner by T. S. Eliot." He
speaks of the novel's "lovely, absurd madness."

Malamud continued to write short stories, finding the form a
constant challenge. The great problem of the short story, as he puts
it, is "to say everything that must be said and to say it quickly,
fleetingly, as though two people had met for a moment in a restaurant, or a railroad station, and one had time only to tell the other they
are both human, and, here, this story proves it." He likes the

challenge of much in little. "And a story must have the right weight of theme," he says, "or it is trivial. If it is too heavy you have something didactic." "The Magic Barrel," published in *Partisan Review* in 1954, attracted more attention than his previous stories had. The extraordinarily fine dialogue, with its strong flavor of Yiddish idiom, the deep feeling of the young rabbinical student, the pathos of the old matchmaker, the delicate approach to fantasy—all these made many people realize that here was an original and powerful talent.

Largely because of "The Magic Barrel," Malamud was awarded a *Partisan Review* Fellowship in 1956, and took his family—he now had two children—to Rome for a year. In part because his wife was of Italian parentage and had relatives in Italy, he made a quick adaptation to his new environment, and some of his most moving stories have grown out of his Italian experience.

Malamud's second novel, *The Assistant,* was published in 1957. In a note for the Norwegian translation he wrote:

> After completing my first novel, *The Natural*, in essence mythic, I wanted to do a more serious, deeper, perhaps, realistic piece of work. The apprentice character interested me, as he has in much of my fiction, the man who, as much as he can in the modern world, is in the process of changing his fate, his life. This sort of person, not at all complicated, appears for the first time in my writing in the short story, "The First Seven Years" (included in my first story collection, *The Magic Barrel*), and I thought I would like to develop the possibilities of his type. . . .

The novel was highly praised, and Malamud was given the Rosenthal Award of the National Institute of Arts and Letters and the Daroff Memorial Award. *The Assistant* has been included in several of the lists of the best ten novels of the past decade that have been appearing in *SR.*

The next year Malamud published a collection of short stories, *The Magic Barrel,* which received the National Book Award. In their citation the judges said: "The fiction prize is awarded to Bernard Malamud for *The Magic Barrel,* a work radiant with personal vision. Compassionate and profound in its wry humor, it captures the poetry of human relationships at the point where imagination and reality meet."

In his acceptance address Malamud tried to make clear what lay behind this book and all his books:

> I am quite tired of the colossally deceitful devaluation of man in this day; for whatever explanation: that life is cheap amid a prevalence of wars; or because we are drugged by totalitarian successes into a sneaking belief in their dehumanizing processes; or tricked beyond self-respect by the values of the creators of our own thing-ridden society; . . . or because, having invented the means of his extinction, man values himself less for it and lives in daily dread that he will in a fit of passion, or pique or absentmindedness, achieve his end. Whatever the reason, his fall from grace in his eyes is betrayed in the words he has invented to describe himself as he is now: fragmented, abbreviated, other-directed, organizational, atonymous man, a victim, in the words that are used to describe him, of a kind of syndechdochic irony, the part for the whole. The devaluation exists because he accepts it without protest.

Malamud refuses to engage in such devaluation, and each story in *The Magic Barrel* is an affirmation of man's ability to realize himself, even in the face of deprivation and disaster.

Malamud spent three and a half years in writing *A New Life*, which was published in 1961. During two of these years, because of a Ford Fellowship, he was able to devote full time to his writing. (He rented a room in Corvallis, where Oregon State College is located, and went there every morning to work). Although it is sometimes assumed that the novel is autobiographical and that Malamud was attacking Oregon State, what has already been said about his career indicates clearly that he is not to be closely identified with S. Levin, probably no more closely than any author is to be identified with any of his heroes. As for Oregon State, he did criticize certain conditions that existed at that institution but because he knew that they existed at other state colleges as well, that this was a national problem. A variety of teachers have written him, saying that he might have been describing the situation they face.

A New Life continues the examination of the apprentice theme present in *The Assistant*. The earlier book describes the conversion of Frank Alpine to the search for the good life, whereas in the latter the conversion has already taken place and the subject is the difficult conduct of the search.

Since finishing *A New Life* and beginning to teach at Bennington College to which he came in 1961, Malamud has spent much of his time in writing short stories, and the fruits of his labor appear in *Idiots First*. He named the volume after the first story it contains to emphasize the theme of the sanctity of human life. As we have seen, he has been greatly troubled by the depreciation of the human in modern times, as terribly exemplified by, though by no means limited to, the Nazi destruction of the Jews. He believes that the human must be protected, and the note that he sounds again and again is compassion.

An Interview with Its Author [*The Fixer*]
Phyllis Meras/1966

From *The Providence Sunday Journal,* 11 September 1966, H9.
Reprinted by permission.

NEW YORK—Bernard Malamud is a slender man, professorial in appearance, with brown eyes behind dark-rimmed glasses. He speaks quickly, but softly, and rarely gestures. For more than 20 years, he has been a teacher of English—at Oregon State College and at Bennington College. This fall he will be a visiting professor at Harvard University.

On a recent visit here, he talked of his fourth, and latest novel, *The Fixer,* and of its origin.

"My last short story," he said, "was something called 'The German Refugee.' It's about a man who has suffered under Hitler and then comes to this country and finds it hard to adjust. It's a story that is both historically and politically centered.

"I decided after that that I wanted to write about politics again—but with a broader base—freedom, injustice, something of that kind. In the beginning, the injustice theme that I had in mind centered around the civil rights movement, and I thought I might write about that. Unfortunately, I lack the experience. But whoever the characters turned out to be, I wanted to write a book giving value to the human being. I think that's particularly important in times like these, when man seems almost in the course of being devalued.

"In many ways, you know, we are becoming a race of automatons—a race in which values other than human are considered the most important. This is a tendency I can feel in the air, and one that I wanted to oppose.

"Then I thought about Caryl Chessman, but I'm not sure there was any injustice in that. It's never been proved, except in the miserable way he was incarcerated. Then I remembered a story my father had told me when I was a boy, about Mendel Beiliss, who was an office manager in a Kiev brick factory at the time of the Tsar, and who was arrested for murder, for ritual purposes, of a Christian boy."

16

This gave Malamud his starting point.

"But I want to emphasize that the book I have written presents a fictional case. I brought in matter from the Dreyfus case, for example, and about Vanzetti when he went mad and was treated at Massachusetts General Hospital, and I put imagination to bear on it all. I wanted to be sure, all the time, that I didn't have the history leading me around by the nose—and sometimes it tried to."

What Malamud was hoping to achieve was the transformation of the original story into mythology, so that although the novel is concerned specifically with a man falsely accused of a murder in Russia in the last century, it also is concerned with the fate of the Jews under the Nazis, and of Negro-Americans today.

He commented that this is the first time that he has written about a period before his own life span (he is 52) and a place with which he is not familiar.

"Usually, I am familiar with what I write about in more ways than just hearsay and reading. Generally, ideas come to me as the result of my own experience, although sometimes weird things simply pop into my mind. Sometimes I think that if you are a writer, you have within you something that entices a story—that knows and attracts the ideas you can use. But this was a different case, and I find the way that it happened rather exciting. Here was an idea carried around from Russia in my father's memory. It was told to me, and I, as an American writer, created it."

Although he has since been to Russia, he had not been when *The Fixer* was written.

"The old Russia I created was an educated guess and the writer's invention, I suppose, and then there were some details that I found in Russian literature—in 'The Steppe' of Chekhov, for example. We writers, you know, live and grow on the literature of the past. When I finally got to Kiev I was curious to see if it was like what I had imagined. I was pleased to see that my version would pass."

Now that the novel is completed—it took him about three years—Mr. Malamud expects to return to writing short stories, which, he says happily, only take a month or two.

"My rhythm has usually been to do a novel, then a handful of short stories, then back to a novel."

Malamud writes every day. "What I write is always absolutely sequential. I have a certain obsessive quality that keeps me directly on the task as it progresses." He is married, and the father of two children—a son at Yale University—and a daughter he hopes will be attending school in Cambridge this fall. What school, he declines to say, in a superstitious and fatherly way, until she has actually entered.

Frequently described as representative of the Jewish school of writers, Malamud decries such classification, and, indeed, questions the existence of such a school.

"I think it's absolutely fascinating and quite strange that one of the things that has happened in American literature since the end of World War II has been the development of a whole group—I say 'group' not 'school'—of gifted Jewish-American writers. I don't think this is a school because I find no common ideology. Sometimes there is Jewish subject matter; sometimes not. But all are certainly different—Bellow, Markfield, Mailer, Gold, myself. Why this diverse group has come to imaginative fruition at this particular point, I can't say.

"With me, the effects of Hitler have had some bearing, but I don't know about the others. Hitler made me aware of the Jewish life of the past and the values the Jewish people tried to uphold. I think that one thing that may have been helpful to the American-Jewish writer is that he has not been afraid to make use of his knowledge of another culture. You get richness from experiencing another culture and you give richness to what you are writing in this way."

How does he view *The Fixer?*

"I have the feeling that it is my strongest book so far."

Bernard Malamud

Haskel Frankel/1966

From *Saturday Review*, 9 October 1966, 39-40. Reprinted by permission of Omni Publications International Ltd.

Bernard Malamud: He is a slight man, bald on top with graying temples. From his crisp attitude, horn-rimmed glasses, and dark olive suit you would suspect that Bernard Malamud was a minor executive in a high-pressure industry somewhere along Madison Avenue. Only his long, slender fingers, which occasionally flash gracefully into the air to underline a point, suggest anything of the sensitivity behind the self-contained, self-assured facade Bernard Malamud brings to an interview. "It's your baby," he said. "You ask 'em and I'll tell 'em."

For the record, Bernard Malamud was born fifty-two years ago in Brooklyn, New York. He took his Bachelor's degree at the City College, his M.A. at Columbia University. He has been on the faculty of Bennington College in Vermont since the fall of 1961. During 1966–67 he will lecture at Harvard. "I'll only be teaching a short story course there. At Bennington I conduct a number of courses. Bennington is extraordinary. The teacher can select the authors he will teach. For example, for Contemporary Fiction I chose such authors as Fitzgerald, Hemingway, Baldwin, and Flannery O'Connor. No, not my own work. I teach myself almost never. An author cannot dictate the total meaning of his work to a classroom.

"I want to say this about *The Fixer*. The story of Yakov Bok, the fixer, is an imaginative piece of work. I don't want it tied to the Beiliss case. *The Fixer* is not factual reportage. As a writer I seek the imaginative fact. You can't make a thing more real than it is but you can make it seem more real through the imaginative fact. For example, Russian friends told me that the Russians didn't treat prisoners as badly as Yakov is treated. That's all right. I was dis-inventing history to give it a quality it didn't have.

"Somewhere along the line, what had happened in Nazi Germany began to be important to me in terms of the book, and that is part of Yakov's story. The Dreyfus case is there, too. There were rumors that

Dreyfus would escape through the aid of Jewish forces. To prevent that, they actually built a wall around his cell and placed a guard in the cell with Dreyfus. From that came the idea of Yakov in chains, something that didn't happen to Mendel Beiliss. You see, for me, the book has a mythological quality. It has to be treated as a myth, an endless story, more than a case study. A case study couldn't be art.

"One of the things I think of now is the Negro, the Negroes who live lives of second-class citizens. Their story is one leading up to a situation that is revolutionary—call it Black Power if you wish. Our country is lucky if this slow blood-letting, these riots that come and then disappear, are all we have to pay for what has happened to the Negro. If the Negroes' story today is revolutionary, Yakov's is pre-revolutionary. Vanzetti went mad and was confined to Massachusetts General; I incorporated that into Yakov. When I leave him, he is at the next step to commitment. The reason is that he has suffered injustice. What has happened to Yakov and how he changes is the story. But what happens to Yakov after I leave him, I don't know.

"As a writer I want uncertainty. It's part of life. I want something the reader is uncertain about. It is this uncertainty that produces drama. Keep the reader surprised. That is enormously important to me. A good writer is an imaginative writer.

"I'll tell you this: if this book isn't about freedom, I don't know what it is about. Every man must be political or where is your freedom?

"*The Fixer* took me two-and-a-half to three years to write. I read for a half year in the field before the first draft, and at intervals after. I did the first draft for details and place and to develop characters and to try an ending. The second draft was to achieve a better and more articulate form, to fulfill a meaning, to enrich the characters and the theme. The third draft tended to eliminate unnecessary and ineffective material, and to heighten the style. It's the first time I have done three drafts.

"I was somewhat doubtful and a little fearful when I began writing it. After all, I was concerned with a time and place I had never experienced. I went on because of some short stories I had written that were fantasy. I thought that if I could make the fantasy world real, then I could make Yakov's world real. Halfway through the second draft (my wife and I were in Europe—a chateau in France, no less) I decided to spend two weeks in Moscow, Kiev, and Leningrad to see what I might have misrepresented in the writing. I wasn't comfortable until I visited the Podol district in Kiev. There I felt I had it made; I hadn't lied. Except for one paragraph, the book stayed as it was.

"I'll tell you something. The title—once you make it part of a Russian setting, it becomes almost a Russian word, yes? Well, it came to me from Corvallis, Oregon; I taught at Oregon State College before going to Bennington. There was a sign I would see almost every day—'Jim the Fixer.' That's where the title came from. Now, you've got an exclusive. I haven't told that to anyone else. Okay?

"Let's end it with this: My work, all of it, is an idea of dedication to the human. That's basic to every book. If you don't respect man, you cannot respect my work. I'm in defense of the human. If you want to say that, that's it.

"My place in literature? It's a phenomenon of time, depending on the quality of my work as I continue to write."

The Man Behind *The Fixer*

Harold Hughes/1966

From *The Oregonian,* 9 October 1966, 8, 21. Copyright © by
The Oregonian Publishing Company. Reprinted by permission.

The Fixer, a new novel that is exciting international criticism, has a
czarist Kiev setting, a Jewish protagonist and a universal theme—but
its title is pure Corvallis, Oregon.

Hardly any two places in the world would seem as far apart in
time, space and thought as Kiev and Corvallis. But are they
strangers?

Bernard Malamud, the author, found the title of his new and fourth
novel while teaching at Oregon State College during the years 1949
to 1961, where he wrote his third novel, *A New Life.*

"JIM THE FIX'R" was the name of a real place that Malamud saw
almost daily in Corvallis and gave the author the idea for the book's
title. In the novel, Yakov Bok, more carpenter than a handyman, is
known as "The Fixer," because that is what he is.

Although none of the characters in the book considers Bok a
"fixer" in the derogatory political sense, the reader might reflect that
in a higher political sense, Bok helps fix the body politic in its struggle
against ignorance, stupidity and prejudice toward the freedom of
man.

Malamud is saying in *The Fixer* that a man ignores politics at his
own peril.

Bok says in the midst of being taken to a stacked trial for a crime
he did not commit:

"One thing I've learned," he thought, "there's no such thing as an
unpolitical man, especially a Jew."

This was also said some 300 years before Christ. "Man is by
nature a political animal," is the way Aristotle put it. Malamud,
speaking recently in an age when some anthropologists say they
would drop the word "political" from the Aristotle statement, sticks
with Aristotle.

Malamud, born in Brooklyn, likes Oregon. This year he is teaching a course in the short story at Harvard University. He left Oregon in 1961 for Bennington College in Vermont. At Harvard he does not lecture about his own work.

He believes that authors cannot do a good job of telling a classroom the meaning of their own works, in the critical sense.

Malamud is a slightly built sensitive man, but his manner and conversation are those of an outward-going "take charge" character who pops names and numbers out of his head with the authority and confidence of a good advertising salesman.

In his conversations with this writer, via telephone from Cambridge, Mass., Malamud exhibited the same warm, crisp style of talking that marks his writings. Asked if he saw any political similarities between Kiev and Corvallis, he quickly made it clear that he found no parallel, no reason to compare the narrow political thought of a czarist Kiev with the free society of a small town in Oregon.

But in *A New Life,* a novel critical of the lack of dedication to scholarship of the English department at Oregon State, the "politics of the English department foretold a deeper involvement in *The Fixer,*" he said.

"That man is by nature political, sometimes gets lost in the shuffle of daily living," Malamud said.

"But I wouldn't want anybody to get any idea that Corvallis or the faculty are not politically concerned," he added.

He said the lack of concern he saw at OSU during the late 1950's was for the humanities and has largely been changed for the better.

Since going to Bennington College to teach, Malamud has returned to visit Corvallis. "My wife and our two children spent a whole summer there in 1963. We have many warm and close friends, and we expect to continue to visit Oregon," he said.

In *A New Life* there was considerable bed-hopping among faculty members. One English professor put a sign on his door after the book came out. It told the tittering students who read the novel, "It wasn't my wife."

Malamud said he tried to mix up the characters of numerous faculty members, "but they did later play a parlor game of 'who's who?' and there was some resentment, but far less than I expected."

The faculty people were most understanding and defended the

book's literary and artistic merits, both in writing and on television, he reported.

There is evidence that somewhat the same willingness to see autobiographical relationships has risen with *The Fixer.*

As a fact of history back in 1911, Mendel Beiliss, Jewish Kiev brickyard worker and father of five children, was charged in a wave of anti-Semitism with the ritualistic murder of a 12-year old boy, whose body was found in a cave. Beiliss was held prisoner, but not thought to have been mistreated, for two years before being brought to trial and found innocent. The case was a pre-revolutionary cause celebre throughout much of Russia and has been little known to the Western world.

In Malamud's new book, Yakov Bok is a childless Jewish brickyard worker whose wife has run off with another man. Yakov is accused of murdering a 12-year old boy whose stabbed body was found in a cave. The Black Hundreds, a kind of Russian Ku Klux Klan, sought to build up anti-Semitic feelings against the Jews by forcing a confession from Yakov that he committed a ritualistic crime and used the child's blood to make a passover Matzo cake. Yakov was held in prison and tortured, but the book ends before he comes to trial.

The Fixer is a novel about one man's submitting to hopeless suffering rather than betray Russia's two million Jews and bring on their heads a ruthless pogrom. If Malamud is saying anything, he is declaring that the freedom of all men depends on the freedom of the least of men—even one who is born a loser and knows it.

"This is an imaginative piece of work," Malamud said, in insisting it is not just a piece of reportage of the Beiliss case.

On several occasions Malamud said, "I was dis-inventing history." He said, "I was trying to move from history to mythology," to write a "gutsy, triumphant book, not a book about defeat and sorrow."

The Fixer, he said, "must be treated as an endless story" and "more than a case study. A case study couldn't be art."

Almost to a man, the important critics have agreed that Malamud has written a work of art. Granville Hicks in the *Saturday Review* said he didn't see how there could be any argument that "it is one of the finest novels of the postwar period."

Robert Scholes in the *New York Times Book Review* made a strong case for his view of it as a "great novel."

The 52-year old Malamud, at the height of his powers and long a writer's kind of writer, calls *The Fixer* "the best book I ever wrote."

And Malamud is the author of some fine books, and one of them, *The Assistant* is a classic to most American writers. *The Magic Barrel* won the National Book Award in 1959, and it was a story, not a novel. [sic] Another of his four novels was *The Natural,* the first of the four he has written.

The Malamud style is crisp, lean and hungry—it eats into your guts.

The fixer says of himself, "I fix what is broken—except in the heart."

He says bitterly of his unfaithful wife who shared his misfortunes, "What she caused she shared." And later of her, "I was afraid she would rub my nose in my future."

Of Kiev, "It is a dangerous city full of churches and anti-Semites."

Again, Yakov, a simple man only slightly exposed to learning and philosophers, declares, "There are no wrong books. What's wrong is the fear of them."

Of his bleak past, he says, "The past is a wound in the head."

And Harry Truman and Nikita Khrushchev might have co-authored: "If you're afraid of the flood stay away from the water."

And, Yakov, refusing to confess to a crime he didn't do says, "If there was no fowl, there are no feathers."

And Malamud, involved in a theme that runs through the Dreyfus case to Sacco and Vanzetti to civil rights and "Black Power," has a Russian Magistrate say: "There's something cursed, it seems to me, about a country where men have owned men as property. The stink of that corruption never escapes the soul, and it is the stink of the future evil."

The "Future Evil," in Russia was its revolutionary excesses. The "future evil" in America has begot the frightful civil rights clashes one hot summer after another.

By both Aristotle and Malamud's own definition, *The Fixer* is a political novel.

"But I have not become a political novelist," Malamud said.

The author, either in the classrooms or in a long-distance interview, is an articulate talker. Not all writers talk well, legend spinners say.

But Malamud talks of ideas and techniques. He is concerned that his books be exciting. If he were a dramatist, he would want them to "play well" and be "good theatre."

Uncertainty, he said, is necessary to the reader.

"It is this uncertainty that produces drama," he said recently, advising writers to "keep readers surprised," adding, a "good writer is an imaginative writer."

Some critics of *The Fixer* feel that while it excels in a polished and disciplined style, that it lacks the great sweep of characters, the sense of drama piled on drama that pour forth from the "big novels."

The Fixer runs only 335 pages. This should not be counted against it. It is not about America, nor is it about American expatriates. It does not experiment with the novel form. It tells a straightforward story. There are no long flashbacks, no side trips into the lives of minor characters.

The reader hardly leaves the side of Yakov Bok, even when Yakov begins to lose his mind and has an imaginary conversation with Nicholas II, the last of the Russian czars.

Malamud has his story and his characters under tight control. He never loses them, as his protagonist lost his way to the Oregon Coast in *A New Life*.

The smell of Mother Russia is on all the pages of *The Fixer*. Malamud researched the people and the period so well, that although he did not visit Kiev until he had finished his last draft, he found it necessary to change only a few lines about the city.

Here is evidence that fiction in the hands of the skilled writer is more true than truth—that facts without man's instincts for the rightness of things are no more than "case histories" or computer readouts, valuable for bridge building but less valuable in explaining the Builder.

Yakov, on the way to his trial, hears the chairman of the jury say:

"None of us are gentry or educated folk, but neither are we without a bit of experience in the world. A man learns to recognize the truth even if he doesn't live by it. And there are times he does if it suits his fancy. The officials may not want us to know what the truth is but it comes in, you might say, through the chinks in the walls."

And Malamud, distrustful of case histories, has found that if you dis-invent history, that truth will come in through the chinks in the walls.

The Book-Makers

Ruth Ingliss/1967

From *Nova*, 17 August 1967, 16.

He is one of the finest living American writers. He probably wouldn't
disagree. For Bernard Malamud, the creator of frightened losers,
endlessly victimised little men, is no frightened little man himself in
spite of his modest, scholarly appearance. When I met him at his
literary agent's office off Bond Street, he greeted me solemnly with
the air of a college professor consenting to discuss worthy literature—
in this case his own.

As *The Fixer*, the story of the pointless persecution of a Jewish
handyman in Czarist Russia some fifty years ago, had climbed and
settled into the British best-seller lists, he thought I'd come to discuss
Yakov Bok, his latest martyr.

Perversely, I really hoped to find out more about my two favour-
ites, Freeman and Fidelman, those two Jewish American boys from
the Bronx whose farcical, comic, sad adventures in Europe thread
their way through his short stories, some of the most brilliant since
Chekhov.

Malamud himself had been a gawky, rather eaglet-like Jewish boy
from Brooklyn and had lived for years in Italy. Were his characters,
fighting their battles against bullies, ridicule and suckerdom, per-
petual prey for luscious, cultured and cruel European women, in any
way reflections of his own experiences?

He looked irritated and passed a hand over his balding head which
glistened in the dull light of the book-lined study where we sat. He
put his fingertips together, retrieving his patience, a long-suffering
academic, used to idiotic questions.

"My works are acts of imagination," he said tersely. "I am not an
art student, nor am I a Russian prisoner under the Czar. It amuses
me that I myself can sound like more than one person. I heard myself
on the radio recently and I sounded like an Englishman." He gave a
wintry smile.

I asked him if you could call Fidelman and Freeman, the buffoons abroad, comic versions of Yakov Bok, as in a sense they were also victims of the world's intolerance.

"Well, I suppose you could say that since all life is victimisation all of us are victims. But I'm not here to push metaphors. My characters aren't Everyman. They are often called clown-victims, the *schlemiels*. This I object to.

"They may seem weak, like Yakov Bok, but they can undergo the most excruciating experiences and come out better at the end."

I thought of Arthur Fidelman again, the nerve-racked, nearly impotent lover of the disdainful religious fanatic, Annamaria, triumphing at the end, an unlikely bed-victor. Annamaria deserved less. Malamud's big dark eyes glowed with interest in this character; his creations are intensely real to him.

"Annamaria went into art to prove something to herself, which is no way to go about it. I'm going to write another Fidelman story this autumn. It will be my sixth. I'm going to Venice to write it. It'll be about how not to become an artist. I'm glad to get down to comedy again after three years in jail."

He spoke of "getting down to comedy" mournfully, as if he meant he were going to take up laying railways. Shuddering a little, he spoke of the three years he had spent in a small office at Bennington writing *The Fixer*. Clearly, it had become Yakov Bok's prison. Beneath his cool, rather superior exterior, one senses that his intensity and identification with his characters make his writing life as uncomfortable as a vat of boiling oil.

"I know that some say Bok is a Christ figure," he said, returning to the creation he seems to love best, "but anyone who is unjustly tormented becomes Jesus."

The theme is sad—Malamud's long, thin bespectacled features, incongruous above a natty tweed sports jacket, matched it in melancholy. After we parted it struck me that this great comic writer had not laughed once in the entire hour.

Malamud Explains Jewish Contribution to U.S. Writing

Shlomo Kidron/1968

From *The Jerusalem Post Week-End Magazine,* 1 April 1968, 13.
Reprinted by permission.

They crowded the aisles in the Jerusalem Khan on Sunday evening to hear Bernard Malamud read his short stories. Hebrew-speaking students, veteran Anglo-Saxon Jerusalemites, many young recent arrivals and the Mayor of Jerusalem sat gripped in complete silence while the leading American Jewish writer's voice filled the hall for two hours. He is here on a two-week visit as guest of the Merkaz Latefutsot.

Telling his audience that he was reading in celebration of Jerusalem, the "thriving, vibrating, beating city of our people," he read "The Jew Bird," "The German Refugee" (written in 1963–4, it preceded *The Fixer* and was the first time he had handled anything remotely historical), "My Son the Murderer" (a short story based on the reaction of American students to the Vietnam war to be published later this year). When Mr. Malamud had finished the audience clapped enthusiastically but sat rooted to their seats as if transfixed by a hypnotist, hoping for more. They were not disappointed. He read "Black is My Favourite Colour" a story dealing with Negro animosity for a white man who falls in love with a black girl.

The underlying symbolism of these stories is inevitably Jewish. Does this classify Bernard Malamud as a "Jewish writer?" The question of the American Jewish writer was the subject of a lecture Mr. Malamud delivered last week to a seminar group studying the Jewish writer in contemporary literature at the Hebrew University and other students able to get into the crowded lecture hall.

Mr. Malamud explained that he himself did not see a "school" of American Jewish writers. The large number of Jews writing in America during the past 30 years share a common fund of Jewish experience and possibly share an interest in the ethical approach, but there is nothing cohesive about their approach to their subjects.

29

Some say "yes" to Jewish life and tradition, some say "no." They are all handling basically American themes which are only sometimes Jewish. Writers like Salinger are not concerned with Jewish subject matter, but this does not mean that they deny their Jewishness, rather they are not writing about what they do not know.

What has made the Jewish writers conspicuous in American literature is their sensitivity to the value of man. The Jew has always considered morality of special significance and the treatment of Judaism as something more than a Jewish experience has transcended his experience as man, Mr. Malamud said. Personally, he was handling the Jew as a symbol "of the tragic experience of man existentially. I try to see the Jew as universal man. Every man is a Jew though he may not know it. The Jewish drama is prototypic, a symbol of the fight for existence in the highest possible human terms. Jewish history is God's gift of drama."

There are many other aspects of the Jew which have made him subject matter for so many writers in America today. There is his role as defender of minority rights, which has been reflected in the part they have taken in the fight for civil rights of the American Negroes. There are the large number of Jewish youth rebelling against the war in Vietnam. There is the effect of the recent Jewish past, the concentration camps, the Nazi Holocaust, which are experiences available to those who lived the drama of what happened in those times.

There is also Israel. The emergence and development of the State of Israel has created a new picture of the Jew. And there are so many things in Israel Americans feel they share. Those who have lived the American adventure see this land as an adventure too. They share a common idea of the seeking of a frontier and a wholeness of the land. There is also the sense of being a melting-pot nation. In the opening, he had said that he was "glad to be in this magic country" (this is his first visit), saying that by this he meant that he saw Israel as "a triumph of human imagination." It was Thursday, the day of Israel's action against Fatah bases across the Jordan, and helicopters carrying the wounded frequently flew over the campus on the way to and from the Ein Karem Medical Centre. And Mr. Malamud added, after a helicopter had passed as he was speaking of "magic" and "imagination": "Though, when you hear the helicopters overhead you realize that something else is needed, too."

However, Israel also symbolizes "the tragedy of the victories—the victory that is never final."

Perhaps more than anything that has made the Jewish writers most prominent in America is the role of Jewish editors, critics and teachers. Magazines such as *Partisan Review* and *Commentary* have encouraged young Jewish writers to publish. Mr. Malamud himself first published in these magazines although he sold his very first story, however, to *Harper's Bazaar.*

Summing up, Mr. Malamud felt that the new conditions created for and by Jews in America, the large percentage of Jews at universities, the large number of Jewish intellectuals in America have all helped to influence American literature during the past generation and to make the role of the Jew prominent.

For Malamud It's Story

Israel Shenker/1971

Bernard Malamud is no procrastinator. "The idea is to get the pencil moving quickly," he said. "Once you've got some words looking back at you, you can take two or three—or throw them away and look for others. I go over and over a page. Either it bleeds and shows it's beginning to be human, or the form emits shadows of itself and I'm off. I have a terrifying will that way."

Nothing about this willful, 57 year old author looks terrifying. We were in the study of his white frame house in Vermont. As I wrote (and the words looked back at me) Malamud seemed content to be talking rather than writing. His desk was covered with manuscript pages. A bookcase lined one wall, and a window looked out on a well-kept lawn.

"Schiller would pull out a drawerful of rotting apples," Malamud said, "The smell got him started. Some take a swig or two. With me it's retype a page of yesterday's material. Then, if it's a good day, I'm off." Until a few years ago, he would write four hours in the morning, two in the afternoon. He has given up work in the afternoon. Instead he listens to records, reads, walks—or plays a game of lawn bowls with his son or daughter or resident guest.

He has a hunger to achieve order for the day. "What would throw me would be a day when I had planned to write and couldn't. So it isn't 'O God, I'm writing!' but 'O God, I'm not writing.' "

An average day ends with half a page, a page, occasionally two. "Sometimes you hit it big and knock off five pages," he said. "Usually dialogue."

For Malamud, fiction is an effort of the imagination to create a world, not simply recall it.

"Sometimes I'll start a first draft to see if it'll go anywhere. If, after a short journey, it looks meager, I won't go on. I don't, as a rule, start a novel without a body of prior experience—a richness of notes that gives me enough to work with and enrich further.

"With me it's story, story, story. Writer's who can't invent stories often pursue other strategies, even substituting style for narrative. I feel that story is the basic element of fiction—though that idea is not popular with disciples of the 'new novel.' They remind me of the painter who couldn't paint people, so he painted chairs.

The story will be with us as long as man is. You know that, in part because of its effect on children. It's through story they realize that mystery won't kill them. Through story they learn they have a future."

Malamud always wanted to be a writer. The first story he remembers writing was about Roger Williams and a bear. In 1940, he got a job teaching at Erasmus Hall Evening High School in Brooklyn, the same high school he had attended as a boy. He subsequently taught for a dozen years at Oregon State University. "I wrote four books in Oregon—*The Natural, The Assistant, The Magic Barrel,* and *A New Life.* And I've done four since then: here at Bennington, two years visiting at Harvard, and back at Bennington." Since 1968, he has worked mostly on a quarter schedule—teaching at Bennington College from March through June, living in Bennington through the summer, then back to Manhattan.

"As you write you talk to yourself and the reader listens. And as you talk to the reader you listen. If you're willing to be discomfited, you can find out who you are and what your writing is. In the beginning it's easy to fool yourself—to think you're doing things you can't do. Wrestling with illusions is part of writing. Invent illusion, and you murder it.

"From book to book there's a difference in subject matter. A difference, too, in comprehension of life—all of this, one would hope, opening and enlarging one's work. One wants to write better and better books. So a writer takes chances that may or may not pay off. He's dead if he doesn't."

In *The Tenants,* Malamud essays a new construction, a new tone, a new theme. He would be unhappy to have the book described simply as a story of black-white relations. He thinks of *The Tenants* as a sort of Prophetic warning against fanaticism. "The book," he says, "argues for the invention of choices to outwit tragedy."

Malamud takes it for granted that a white writer can portray aspects of black experience. "If I'm not afraid to invent God in my fiction—or kinds of Jews I've never met—I don't see why I shouldn't invent Willie Spearmint. Willie is singular." He is not meant to be universal anything.

Usually, Jewish experience has been what some readers could rely on in Malamud's work. "I write about Jews because I know something about them and they move me," he said. "I don't live a Jewish life in the religious sense, though I have been influenced by their concern with morality.

"Another thing that has caused me to be concerned with Jewish subject matter is the fact that I'm married to a Gentile. This made me ask myself what it is I'm entitled to in Jewish experience. In fiction, I'm not afraid to go from Jewish experience to non-Jewish experience.

"Through her family my wife opened Italian life to me. Her background is richly Italo-American. When we lived in Rome, I fell into Italian family life there."

Malamud: *The Tenants* is a tight, tense book. It's closer to the quality of short fiction. There's less of the kind of personality that would be associated with a Malamud character.
Interviewer: What is a Malamud character?
Malamud: *Oi vey.*
Interviewer: A man who says *'Oi vey'?*
Malamud: He has his reasons.
Interviewer: Doesn't everybody?
Malamud: That's the point. A Malamud character is someone who fears his fate, is caught up in it, yet manages to outrun it. He's the subject and object of laughter and pity.

"I'm not competing for the heavyweight title," Malamud said. "That was Papa's bag. I'm struggling to say it as well as I can—in a way I haven't said it before. Art lives on surprise. A writer has to surprise himself to be worth reading."

For Malamud there is always the temptation to rewrite once again. "But I know it's finished when I can no longer stand working on it. Valéry said that a work of art is never completed—it's abandoned. He'd leave his manuscript where a friend could find it and cart it off to the publisher. I'm content to part with my manuscript when it's ready to walk away."

An Interview with Bernard Malamud

Leslie and Joyce Field/1973

From *Bernard Malamud: A Collection of Critical Essays.* Edited
by Leslie A. Field and Joyce W. Field. Englewood Cliffs, N.J.:
Prentice-Hall, 1975 pp. 8-17. Reprinted by permission of Leslie
and Joyce Field.

The following commentary and summary from an exchange of letters
between Mr. Malamud and the interviewers from May 11, 1973 to
August 2, 1973 reveal the nature and scope of this interview.

We wrote Mr. Malamud asking him to agree to an interview
because even though his fiction is the important thing, we felt that a
full-scale interview could contribute a great deal also. His response to
a variety of questions would, we believed, be most helpful to readers,
students, critics, and scholars.

Ours was a simple plan. We would spend a few hours with Mr.
Malamud taping questions and answers. We would then send him
transcripts of the tape and he would modify as he saw fit—to best
reflect what he wanted to say at any given point. Our object was
simply to get a straightforward series of responses to questions often
asked about his fiction. But we left other options open. For example,
perhaps he would choose to do all of this by mail rather than through
a personal interview.

Mr. Malamud chose the mail interview route. He pointed out that
in the past he had avoided most interviews, "especially when tape
recorders are relentlessly present," because he was often unhappy
with his own responses. He added that he dislikes explaining his
fiction because by describing his "intent" he may in effect "betray"
his work. He fears that people may substitute what he says about his
writing for their own imaginative reading of his fiction. Thus a certain
kind of interview could be self-defeating.

Mr. Malamud went on to say that he doesn't "like to say where
stories originated, from what incident, real or imagined, from my life
or anyone else's." He felt strongly that one shouldn't confuse the
author's life with his fiction or even devote much effort to relating the
two—"That's a critic's pleasure and not mine."

When the questions were sent to Mr. Malamud, we emphasized that we had tried to follow certain guidelines, some of which he himself had proposed. We would use only those questions which had been asked in one way or another by readers, critics, students. We would try to avoid questions addressed to specific interpretations of his works, his characters. We would also try to avoid belaboring him with queries about sources. And, finally, we would try to eliminate personal matters.

We realized that we hadn't succeeded on all counts. However, we asked him to answer those questions he felt he could answer as completely as possible. He had the choice of answering part of a question rather than the whole. Or he could modify certain questions before he answered. In a word, we wanted him to be comfortable in his approach and to feel free to tailor the whole to suit his needs.

For the most part, the questions appear here as they were originally presented to Mr. Malamud. One question was eliminated. The one on baseball was recast by him, and he revised one of his answers. At his suggestion, a summary of our correspondence was used rather than a verbatim transcript of the letters. Finally, we believe we exercised our best editorial judgment in shortening a few questions when the answers were received.

The Fields: It has been reported that you once said: "A Malamud character is someone who fears his fate, is caught up in it, yet manages to outrun it. He's the subject and object of laughter and pity." Could you elaborate on this statement? Do you still consider that it capsulizes recent important Malamud characters—for example, Fidelman, Yakov Bok, and Harry Lesser?

Malamud: I can't work up any great enthusiasm for the statement but what I imagine it means is that my characters often outwit their predictable fates. I'd say that holds for Fidelman, Yakov Bok, and even Harry Lesser.

The Fields: How did you happen to write a baseball novel?

Malamud: Baseball players were the "heroes" of my American childhood. I wrote *The Natural* as a tale of a mythological hero because, between childhood and the beginning of a writing career, I'd been to college. I became interested in myth and tried to use it, among other things, to symbolize and explicate an ethical dilemma of American life. Roy Hobbs is as American as the White House lawyers involved in Watergate.

Fields: As you know, the "academic novel" has been a subject of critical commentary. It used to be said, for example, that every professor of English had at least one academic novel within him that was crying to get out. Would it be accurate to say that a novel such as *A New Life* (although it obviously does much more than depict academic life) could not be written today because the campus is now a composite of a drastically altered set of symbols?

Malamud: This is an involved query concerning what to me was the simple act of writing a novel out of my experience. The "academic novel," as such, simply doesn't interest me.

The Fields: One fairly popular view has it that the *schlemiel* as metaphor or character in fiction is an uneasy transplant from East European Yiddish fiction to modern American fiction. As a matter of fact, two recent full-length books on the *schlemiel* conclude that the *schlemiel* as fictional character was able to work quite effectively for a Malamud and a Bellow up through the sixties. At that point these critics sound the death knell for the *schlemiel.* They say, for example, that an America which is going through (or has just gone through) Vietnam and civil strife, a country which is no longer considered a "winner," cannot accept with equanimity a fictional depiction of a "loser." How do you react to this commentary on the use of the *schlemiel* in fiction?

Malamud: With many apologies, I don't much care for the *schlemiel* treatment of fictional characters. Willy-nilly, it reduces to stereotypes people of complex motivations and fates—not to mention possibilities. The literary critic who wants to measure the quality and depth of a fictional character has better terms to use.

The Fields: When you received the National Book Award for *The Fixer* you said the novel was not simply a fictional retelling of the Beilis case of Czarist Russia, that it involved much more, that in some way it also owed much to a later horrible event in history—the Nazi Holocaust. Could you elaborate on this? Moreover, do you believe you could have used the Dreyfus case or the Sacco-Vanzetti case to express equally well what it was you had to say in *The Fixer?*

Malamud: My original desire was to write a novel based on the Sacco-Vanzetti case, but when I began to read on the subject I had the feeling that I couldn't invent a more dramatic story than the original. Since I was interested in how some men grow as men in prison I turned to the Beilis case, which my father had told me about when I was a boy. *The Fixer* is largely an invention. That is, I've tried to bring it as close to a folk tale as I could. However, in it I was able to relate feelingfully to the situation of the Jews in Czarist Russia partly because of what I knew about the fate of the Jews in Hitler's Germany.

The Fields: I. B. Singer has said he writes about devils, sprites, and evil spirits—about the supernatural in general—because he believes in the supernatural. Much earlier, Hawthorne explained that he wanted to find some "neutral ground" for his fiction. Your use of the supernatural has been compared to that of Singer and Hawthorne. Do you believe in the supernatural? Do you look for a "neutral ground" in your fiction as you order your supernatural or fantastic worlds? Or do some other explanations apply to this world of your fiction?

Malamud: I don't believe in the supernatural except as I can invent it. Nor do I look for a "neutral ground" for my fiction. I write fantasy because when I do I am imaginative and funny and having a good time.

The Fields: In one of your early, infrequent interviews, we believe you said that Kafka was one of the modern authors who had influenced you. How?

Malamud: He writes well. He moves me. He makes me want to write well and move my readers. Other writers have had a similar effect. I guess what I'm trying to say is that I am influenced by literature.

The Fields: There has been much critical commentary concerning a statement you are alleged to have made: "All men are Jews." Did you ever actually make this statement? Do you believe it is true? It is, of course, a view one cannot take literally. In any event, would you elaborate on the "All men are Jews" statement?

Malamud: I think I said "All men are Jews except they don't know it." I doubt I expected anyone to take the statement literally. But I think it's an understandable statement and a metaphoric way of indicating how history, sooner or later, treats all men.

The Fields: Some have seen parallels between your work and painting, especially the spiral, mystical works of Chagall. This has been observed, for instance, in your short story "The Magic Barrel." Elsewhere readers have remarked on your concern with the plastic arts in general—in *Pictures of Fidelman,* for example. What influence has painting had on your fiction? Have you consciously tried to fuse one art form with another?

Malamud: It's true that I did make use of what might be called Chagallean imagery in "The Magic Barrel." I did so intentionally in that story, but I've not done it again in any other piece of fiction, and I feel that some critics make too much of Chagall as an image maker in my work. Chagall, as a painter, doesn't mean as much to me as Matisse, for instance. Painting helps me to see with greater clarity the multifarious world and to depict it simply.

The Fields: Saul Bellow, Philip Roth, Bruce J. Friedman, and other contemporary American novelists have rejected the label "Jewish-American Writer." In one way or another you have also. Nevertheless, you, the other writers mentioned—and one could bring in additional writers such as Chaim Potok and Herbert Gold—are still being classified as Jewish-American writers by many scholars, critics, and readers. It is our impression that the responsible people who place you and others in this category do not intend to reduce your stature or disregard the universalism they see in your work. They have simply categorized or schematicized as scholars are prone to do, much as one labels Faulkner a Southern-American writer because the spirit of place (the South) imbues his work or Graham Greene an Anglo-Catholic writer because a certain spirit of a specific religion permeates much of his significant work. How do you respond to this categorizing of you and your work? Would you reject the term Jewish-American writer categorically?

Malamud: The term is schematic and reductive. If the scholar needs the term he can have it, but it won't be doing him any good if he limits his interpretation of a writer to fit a label he applies.

Bellow pokes fun at this sort of thing by calling "Bellow-Malamud-Roth" the Hart, Schaffner and Marx of Jewish-American literature.

The Fields: Whether or not you accept the label of Jewish-American writer, would you not agree that your writing reveals a special sense of a people's destiny that more often than not cannot be fully grasped in all its nuances and vibrations by those who are not fully sensitized to that people or its destiny? On one level, for example, it has been said that one must be a Russian in order to respond completely to the nineteenth-century notion of salvation through suffering that is dramatized so well by Dostoevsky. Or that only blacks can truly appreciate the plight of black America. Could one not also say that only those who understand the *Yiddishkeit* of the characters or the Yiddish milieu are able to respond fully to the silent communication between a Morris Bober and a Brietbart or between a Yakov Bok and his father-in-law, and so on?

Malamud: I'm sensitive to Jews and Jewish life but so far as literature is concerned I can't say that I approve of your thesis: that one has to be of a certain nationality or color to "fully grasp" the "nuances and vibrations" of its fiction. I write on the assumption that any one sensitive to fiction can understand my work and *feel* it.

The Fields: Much has been made of the prison motif in your work. Do you see the prison metaphor as one that aptly describes the dilemma of modern man? If so, could you elaborate on this?

Malamud: It's a metaphor for the dilemma of all men throughout history. Necessity is the primary prison, though the bars are not visible to all. Then there are the man-made prisons of social injustice, apathy, ignorance. There are others, tight or loose, visible or invisible, according to one's predilection or vulnerability. Therefore our most extraordinary invention is human freedom.

The Fields: It has been noted that if one is to interpret your work correctly, one must not weigh Judaic interpretations too heavily. One must rather look to the Christian symbolism or perhaps the Judaic-Christian. How do you respond to this?

Malamud: I don't know whether there is a "correct" interpretation of my work. I hope not.

The Fields: You yourself have said that in your fiction you are concerned with humanity, man's humanism. Could you explore this notion somewhat?

Malamud: I don't think I ought to. People can read; they can read what I say. That's a lot more interesting than reading what I say I say.

The Fields: Some have remarked that you are not interested in a novel of ideas as such, but in a depiction of human nature. Henry James, for example, was quite vocal in explaining his fictional approach (which he attributed to Turgenev's influence). That is, he would start out with a clearly defined character thrust into a specific situation. How that character responded to the situation became all-important. Do you believe your own fictional approach follows this Jamesian-Turgenev method?

Malamud: Basically, that's it, but I don't think I would limit my "fictional approach" to the "Jamesian-Turgenev method." One learns from Shakespeare as well. My novels are close to plays. I had once, as a young writer, wanted to be a playwright.

The Fields: The tension between life and art seems to be a major concern in your fiction. One could see it in some of your early work. And as recently as *The Tenants* and *Rembrandt's Hat* it is obvious that this tension is still a significant part of your fiction. Of course *Pictures of Fidelman* is introduced by the epigraphs taken from Rilke and Yeats, and is followed by A. Fidelman's terse conclusion. Many would agree that life versus art is central to the Fidelman stories. Do you concur? Can you perhaps now probe in a bit more detail the life versus art theme as you see it?

Malamud: It isn't life versus art necessarily; it's life *and* art. On Fidelman's tombstone read: "I kept my finger in art." The point is I don't have large thoughts of life versus art; I try to deepen any given situation.

The Fields: As one reads through your work one is tempted to continue pairing concepts, terms such as the life and art mentioned earlier. Another pair—love and redemption—comes to mind. The Frank Alpines and Yakov Boks, for example, apparently do redeem themselves. But terms such as love, humanity, belonging, compassion or *rachmones* or *menschlechkeit* (and other terms as well) seem to slip in and out of one's consciousness in this context. In a variety of ways, you seem to demonstrate that love brings redemption to an individual. But both of these terms—love and redemption—are endowed by you with a multiplicity of meanings. Would this be a fair estimation? Or would you prefer one to place love and redemption into a narrower, perhaps more religious context?

Malamud: Yes, there are various ways. I wouldn't want to place love and redemption in a religious context, although acting out love and redemption may be a religious deed.

The Fields: Characters in your fiction from time to time wrestle with their Jewishness. In response to a question, Morris Bober defines Jewishness. Bok ultimately feels he must rejoin his people. But these characters and others seem to adapt as minority people to the pluralistic societies they find themselves in—whether it be the United States, Russia, or Italy. One of our students recently noted that the current writers who frequently people their work with Jews— Bellow, Roth, I. B. Singer, etc.—and who explore serious matters concerning Jewishness, probe or suggest a variety of possible identities. These may involve religion, assimilation, acculturation, bundism, social action, etc. But Zionism (specifically seeking one's Jewish identity in Israel) is quite conspicuous by its absence. As a matter of fact, this student further observed that the real (in-depth) American Zionist novel has not only *not* been written, but probably will never be undertaken by a major American writer. Do you agree? Why has Zionism played such a minor role for the Jewish characters who have populated so much of our fiction during the last two decades?

Malamud: I agree. Writing about Zionism wouldn't interest me. I'd rather write about Israel if I knew the country. I don't, so I leave it to the Israeli writers.

The Fields: Not too long ago Robert Alter noted the black-white confrontations in *Rabbit Redux, Mr. Sammler's Planet,* and *The Tenants.* In the latter two books, of course, the whites assumed another dimension because they were Jews. It is perhaps no coincidence that these books emerged at a time of great conflict between blacks and whites in this country and in certain pockets of the country between blacks and Jews. Do you yourself see a new relationship developing in the United States between blacks and Jews? If so, how do you define this relationship?

Malamud: It's impossible to predict—it may go one way; it may go another. A good deal depends on the efficacy of American democracy. If that works as it ought—guaranteeing blacks what they deserve as human beings—a larger share of our national wealth, equal opportunity under the law, their rights as men, the relationship of blacks and Jews and other minorities are bound to improve.

The Fields: At one time you mentioned that even though a number of years separate your first Fidelman story from the last one, when you initially created Arthur Fidelman you had plans that went beyond "The Last Mohican." Can you explain why it was that they became a series of separate stories ultimately woven into a novel rather than a novel more in the form of *The Assistant* or *The Tenants?* Also, the name Fidelman. Some critics have played around with the name as symbol. Few, however, have noted that it is also your mother's maiden name. Was this choice significant or incidental?

Malamud: Right after I wrote "The Last Mohican" in Rome in 1957, I worked out an outline of other Fidelman stories, the whole to develop one theme in the form of a picaresque novel. Why do it the same way all the time?

I used my mother's maiden name because I needed a name I liked.

The Fields: Has your wife's Italian background contributed to your "Italian" stories in the same way that your Jewish background has contributed to your "Jewish" stories? We are talking here more of an Italian and Jewish context, characterization, and rhythm of place rather than simply settings and people that happen to be Italian and Jewish.

Malamud: Yes. I met Italians in America through my wife before and after we were married, and because she had been to Italy and could speak Italian like a native, we decided to live in Rome with our children in 1956–7. Through her relatives and acquaintances I was almost at once *into* Italian life and got the feel of their speech, modes of behavior, style. When I go abroad I like to stay in one place as long as possible until I can define its quality.

The Fields: Do you read much of the criticism of your fiction? How do you respond to literary criticism in general?

Malamud: I read here and there in criticism about my work when it hits the eye. I don't go looking for it. I like imaginative interpretations of my books, whether I agree with them or not. I enjoy criticism that views the work in ways I haven't anticipated—that surprises me. I dislike crap—criticism, favorable or unfavorable, that really doesn't understand what the books are about. I do take seriously insightful criticism of individual works that affirm judgments, negative or positive, of my own.

The Fields: Does teaching interfere with your writing of fiction or does it help and complement in some ways?

Malamud: I devote little time to teaching now—a quarter of a program, one class in the spring. Teaching "interferes" only in cutting down writing time. On a day I teach I can't write. But teaching helps more than it hinders. It gets me out of my study and puts me in touch with people. And I like reading, and talking about books.

I'm not arguing that the academic life is the life for a writer—often it restricts experience and homogenizes it; but I am grateful that when I was earning little or nothing as a writer, because of teaching, when I wrote I wrote only what I wanted to write.

The Fields: In *The Assistant* your characters are frequently referred to as *the Poilesheh, the Swede, the Italyener, the Norwegian, the Greek,* and even *the Jew.* In one sense it reminds one of Stephen Crane's use of *the youthful soldier, the cheerful soldier, the loud soldier, the spectral soldier,* etc. Were you attempting an ethnic view of twentieth-century urban America much as Crane may have tried to depict the world of the Civil War Soldier through a set of humors?

Malamud: No, I don't play those games. That's the way the Bobers talk.

The Fields: Another reference to Stephen Crane, a variation. Are you very concerned with drawing prototypes and archetypes in your fiction as opposed to depicting realistic human beings? In other words, do you find yourself deliberately flattening out some of your characters much as a Stephen Crane would do or as a Cézanne would do in painting because you are at times much more interested in something beyond the depiction of a recognizable three-dimensional character?

Malamud: I would never deliberately flatten a character to create a stereotype. Again—I'm not much one for preconceptions, theories— even E. M. Forster's "flats and rounds." Most of all I'm out to create real and passionate human beings. I do as much as I can with a character. I may not show him in full blast *every* moment, but before the end of a fiction he has had a chance to dance his dance.

The Fields: It appears that you rarely develop children or young characters in your fiction, especially in your longer fiction. Children are in the background often in novels such as *The Natural* and *A New Life,* but are almost nonexistent in other works. Have you been conscious of this characteristic of your fiction? Do you have any thoughts on this matter?

Malamud: I've got to leave something for my old age.

The Fields: Would you agree that yours is basically a comic vision of life?

Malamud: There is comedy in my vision of life. To live sanely one must discover—or invent it. Consider the lilies of the field; consider the Jewish lily that toils and spins.

The Fields: Do you see a major shift in the point of view of your recent short stories collected in *Rembrandt's Hat* as opposed to views you may have held when you wrote *The Magic Barrel* and *Idiots First?* There is still, of course, the concern with humanity or *menschlechkeit.* Is there more stoic acceptance in these stories?

Malamud: They're the stories of an older man than the one who wrote *The Magic Barrel* and *Idiots First,* possibly a man who knows more than he did ten or fifteen years ago.

The Fields: Do you read more fiction or nonfiction these days? At any rate, could you give us some notion of your current reading?

Malamud: I read a good deal of biography. I like some of the Latin American novelists I've been reading lately. I read too much half-ass American fiction and not enough good poetry. At the moment I'm rereading *Walden.* I'm also reading Jane Goodall's study of chimps, *In the Shadow of Man.* More than half of my reading centers around what I may need to know for my own writing.

The Fields: Would you say something about your writing habits, the physical setting for your writing, and perhaps along the way give a few clues about your earliest writing experiences, etc.?

Malamud: I've answered this question in an interview with Israel Shenker in the *N. Y. Times.** It's not a question that I love to answer more than once. Young writers have a legitimate but exaggerated interest in the way other writers work. To them I'd say the way to work is the way you write best.

The Fields: You've mentioned another novel you are working on now. Would you care to give us some idea of its direction and scope?

Malamud: I don't believe, as Hemingway seemed to, that you hex a work-in-progress simply by talking about it. I'm writing another novel—a difficult one, just started, which may not see the light of day. If it does, the opening paragraph may read as follows:

"Although it isn't yet end of summer, William Dubin, at one moment of his walk in the country—rural into pastoral—beats his arms vigorously across chest and shoulders as though he had suddenly encountered cold, the clouds have darkened, and a snowstorm threatens. He had, in a way, been thinking of winter."

The Fields: Can you think of other questions which have not been asked or which should be asked or which you would like asked? Perhaps you can supply answers for these unasked questions.

Malamud: No, I've talked too much.

*Reprinted as "Bernard Malamud on Writing Fiction: An Interview by Israel Shenker," *Writer's Digest,* 52:7 (July 1972), 22–23. Appeared originally in *The New York Times,* Oct. 3, 1971, pp. 20, 22.

My Characters Are God-Haunted

Curt Leviant/1974

From *Hadassah Magazine*, 55 (June, 1974), 18-19. Reprinted
with the permission of *Hadassah Magazine* and Curt Leviant.

Bernard Malamud, a central figure in contemporary
American literature, hardly needs an introduction to
American readers. Born in New York in 1914, he was
educated at City College and then devoted himself to
writing and teaching. He is the author of five novels (*The
Natural, The Assistant, A New Life, The Fixer,* and *The
Tenants*) and four collections of short stories (*The Magic
Barrel, Idiots First, Fidelman: An Exhibition,* and *Rembrandt's Hat*). Most of Malamud's heroes are Jews, and
moral and ethical concerns are part of his thematic fabric.

Although he is now working on a new novel, and in any
case rarely gives interviews, Mr. Malamud was kind
enough to consent to this one. He did not want a tape
recorder used and asked that my questions be submitted
in advance so that he might be able to give them proper
thought and reflection.

Since, despite the advance questions, there was a give-
and-take atmosphere—with interjected questions and remarks—and since Malamud's mind and grace of articula-
tion are obviously swifter than my hand-held pen, I was
not able to stenograph his remarks. Hence, in order to
avoid misquoting Mr. Malamud, or attributing remarks in
the absence of tape-recorded fidelity, I should state that
Bernard Malamud's answers are my reconstructions (from
notes)—even the order of responses may have been
slightly altered—and should not be considered direct
quotations or representative of the way Mr. Malamud
speaks. Obviously, however, there are no fictional addi-
tions on my part and no fantasized responses.

Leviant: What sort of Jewish education did you get?

Malamud: First let me give you some background on my parents.
They were born in Russia, the Ukraine—in small towns—and came

to the United States between 1905 and 1910. My father became a grocer and my mother helped him. Because of poor *parnosse* (livelihood) they stayed late in the store—

Leviant: Like Bober in *The Assistant?*

Malamud: Yes . . . My home life, then, was meager. I saw little of them in a family context, even though I helped out in the store when I was in high school. My parents, though sensitive people, were not well educated.

Leviant: But like all Jewish parents they wanted their son to have an education.

Malamud: Of course. There were Yiddish books at home which I was unable to read, and I regret this. In a way I feel I was gypped, just as I was when I didn't have the opportunity of learning music. But my parents did take me to the Yiddish theater. As a child I saw the plays of Sholom Aleichem and Peretz, as well as certain melodramas.

There was also a link between our family and the Yiddish stage. My mother's brother was a *soufflyor* for the Yiddish theater—one who prompts the actors from a booth at the front of the stage—and he managed a Yiddish theatrical troupe, Samuel Goldberg's, when it was on tour in Argentina. My mother also had a cousin, Isador Cashier, a well-known Yiddish actor, who performed in the original production of I. J. Singer's *Yoshe Kalb.*

My father was mildly socialistic and not religious. Usually, there were no synagogues around. So, then, as a combination of these factors, I received little in the way of a Jewish education.

Leviant: Then you never went to *heder* or Talmud Torah?

Malamud: No. I did go to *shul* with friends, but I was unable to read Hebrew. I was also never taught to read Yiddish.

Leviant: But do you understand Yiddish? Can you speak it?

Malamud: I can get along in Yiddish. If in Israel a lady asked me for directions, I could reply, but I can't make my way with more intellectual material. Once, when I was a student at City College, I wanted to go to a Yiddish club to learn Yiddish, but I was talked out of it. I was told to study Hebrew instead.

Leviant: Did you speak Yiddish with your parents?

Malamud: Yes.

Leviant: So then, if you were to learn the Hebrew alphabet—

which would probably take you a day or so—you'd be able to get into Yiddish literature.

Malamud: Very likely.

Leviant: Have you done any reading in classical Hebrew or Yiddish literature in translation?

Malamud: I've read Mendele Mokher Seforim, Sholom Aleichem, Peretz, Sholem Asch and one or two others.

Leviant: Have you read Isaac Bashevis Singer's works?

Malamud: Quite a few books. I came to him rather late.

Leviant: And of Hebrew?

Malamud: I've read Agnon and some of the modern Israeli writers including Mati Megged and Aharon Megged. I've also read Amos Oz.

Leviant: Have you been to Israel? Have you thought of setting a story there?

Malamud: I have visited Israel, but I can't set a story there because I spent only two weeks in Israel.

Leviant: I assume you've been to Russia, because "Man in the Drawer" [about a half-Jewish Russian writer] takes place there.

Malamud: Yes, I have. And look what I found in Moscow, a volume of Jewish stories in English by Ivan Olbracht.

Leviant: Do you feel that you are part of a literary tradition? If so, is it American, Jewish, Western, or a fusion of all of these?

Malamud: A fusion. I've read in all these literatures. A large part of my background is American literature. I've been "influenced" by Hawthorne, Melville, Henry James, Faulkner, Sherwood Anderson, Hemingway, and others whose works I've read with great care and interest. What I mean is that literature in general has influenced me, but American literature in particular. I also know something of the literature of England, France, Italy and Germany, and as I've said, I have read Yiddish literature and seen Yiddish drama.

Leviant: What role does the Jewish tradition play in your work? I note, for instance, that your novel *The Tenants* concludes with the Yiddish phrase "*hob rahmones,*" followed by many lines of the word "mercy."

Malamud: I would say that my subject matter mixes the universal and the particularly Jewish. Some borderline figures in my work act under the influence of their Jewish background. I write about Jews because I know them. I'm comfortable with them. The interest in ethicality by the Jews has always excited me. The struggle against self is a basic struggle. Almost anything one reads touches on this. Also, the history of the Jews is a great drama. Obviously, it's not one of pure darkness. I also like Jewish history as a metaphor for the fate of all men.

There are times when I write about Jews but not about Jewish concerns. I'm interested in literature, profoundly moved by it. I've dedicated my life to it. I am a writer and I write what I know. I write what I have to write. A writer must be free to choose any subject matter.

Leviant: But choosing any subject matter depends on time and circumstances. Abraham Cahan, editor of the *Yiddish Daily Forward,* couldn't get his Jewish-themed work accepted by an American publisher late in the nineteenth century, despite intervention by one of the most influential American writers at the time, William Dean Howells. At that period, publishers simply wouldn't publish a work on a Jewish theme, about Jewish immigrants in New York City.

Malamud: I'm not talking about publication. I'm talking about writing. There are hundreds of Russian writers who write what they please, but only for the drawer.

Leviant: Have your stories been published in the Soviet Union?

Malamud: Yes, they've done a book of my short stories.

Leviant: What besides their names and milieu makes your characters Jewish?

Malamud: Their Jewish qualities, the breadth of their vision, their kind of fate, their morality, their life, their awareness, responsibility, intellectuality, and ethicality. Their love of people and God. Someone said recently that my characters are God-haunted.

Leviant: God-haunted? I had supposed man-haunted was more accurate.

Malamud: There are some characters who strongly believe in God. And let me add that I don't feel inhibited in inventing God-haunted characters, which has nothing to do with whether I am or am not religious.

Leviant: Would you like to speak on how one of your stories came to be written? For instance, "The First Seven Years," or "The Jewbird," or "Man in the Drawer?"

Malamud: I don't like to explain my stories, and as a rule I won't comment on interpretations of my fiction, so that students will feel free to interpret it as they please. I like imaginative interpretations of my books whether I agree with them or not, so long as they are consistent and make sense.

Leviant: If the characters in "Talking Horse" had had general American or, let's say, Irish names, would you have had a different tale?

Malamud: Yes, but I still might have had a Jewish story. Richard Fein, the critic, once wrote that there are three ingredients to a Jewish story. It has to have a horse, a victim, and loose technique. Since "Talking Horse" has all of these, I suppose it may be defined as a Jewish story. However, I don't think that's very important.

Leviant: Why, then, did you choose to make the heroes of "Talking Horse" Jews?

Malamud: Because I write easily of Jews. Of course, "Talking Horse" has some relationship to the Book of Jonah, and also to the Old Testament beyond the Book of Jonah. Incidentally, "Jewbird" [about a talking Jewish bird named Schwartz] led to "Talking Horse," and I plan to do a third story with a talking animal, probably a short novel.

Leviant: Could you categorize your stories as falling into any of these groups: stories from real life, stories spurred by other fiction, stories purely imaginative?

Malamud: A combination of these.

Leviant: There is obviously much blending, but could you give an example from your writing of any of these categories? For instance, I have in mind "Silver Crown," in your latest book of stories, *Rembrandt's Hat*. Wasn't that story based on a news item, late in 1972, I believe, that two hasidic faith healers had been arrested in the Bronx for conning Jews out of their money with false promises of miracles?

Malamud: Yes, it was taken from *The New York Times*. However, all the characters are mine.

Leviant: In one of Hawthorne's prefaces, he defines romance as "a neutral territory somewhere between the real world and the fairyland, where the actual and the imaginary meet." Elsewhere, he states that romance is a piece of writing "wherein the author mingles the marvelous rather as a slight, delicate evanescent flavor . . . in which there is some legendary mist which the reader may either disregard . . . or allow it to float imperceptibly for the sake of picturesque effect." Can this version of romance as a genre of fiction be applied to your stories?

Malamud: I believe that the link with Hawthorne exists, and so does one with Henry James, which critics recently commented on.

Leviant: What foreign authors do you like?

Malamud: Borges, Marquez, Böll, Gunter Grass, some of Solzhenitsyn, some of Jean Genet.

Leviant: Do you do much rewriting, as Isaac Babel is said to have done: fifty versions of one short story, each version getting progressively shorter. Or do you work like Joyce Carol Oates, who conceives a work of fiction, then types it up rapidly without changing a word?

Malamud: I am a rewriter. I rewrite a number of times. Imaginative richness is born in rewriting.

Leviant: Thomas Mann and Shmuel Yosef Agnon set rigorous writing schedules for themselves. Of Agnon it was known in Israel that one dare not call him in the morning, because he did not like to be disturbed during his morning writing. Do you have a vigorous schedule of this sort? I recall reading years ago in *The New York Post*—I think this was when you were at the University of Oregon— that you taught three days a week and wrote three days a week.

Malamud: Yes, I write mostly in the morning. I used to teach half a week and write half a week but now I write six out of seven days.

Leviant: Have your stories been translated widely?

Malamud: Into twenty-one languages in all, including a story into Chinese.

Leviant: Nationalist Chinese or Communist Chinese?

Malamud: Taiwan. I'm also translated and footnoted in Japanese. In one footnote, the translation of *Gottenyu* [dear God] came out as "God damn you!"

Leviant: When did you first begin to write? Where were you first published?

Malamud: I began writing when I was a kid in grammar school in Brooklyn. My first commercially published story appeared in *Harper's Bazaar* in 1950.

Leviant: Did the movie versions of your novel *The Fixer* and your short story "Angel Levine" live up to your expectations?

Malamud: Where the films have failed, the original scripts were bad. There is very little that a director can do to make a bad script good.

Leviant: Are you writing any plays?

Malamud: No.

Leviant: Do you read reviews and criticism of your works? And are you affected intellectually by such criticism?

Malamud: I read here and there. I don't go looking for it. I enjoy views that surprise me, but I dislike prosaic evaluation. However, I do take seriously insightful criticism, whether the judgments are negative or positive.

Leviant: Some of your magnificent end-lines sound as though they might have been the spurs to the entire story. (For example, the first epigraph in *Rembrandt's Hat:* "And an old white horse galloped away in the meadow" is by T.S. Eliot.) Have you ever constructed a story from an end-line?

Malamud: Yes, I have had experience of this sort. However, I reread the line from Eliot's "Journey of the Magi" after "Talking Horse" had been written.

Leviant: Have you ever used your own fiction in your classes?

Malamud: Never. And I have no intention of doing so.

Leviant: Which is your favorite work among your own fiction?

Malamud: I really have none, although there is some tendency to favor one's early work.

Leviant: Do you see an inner cohesiveness, a miniature world, in your works—as for instance the world of Faulkner, or the world of Sholom Aleichem—with an ethos all its own?

Malamud: I like to be told that I've created a world.

The Art of Fiction: Bernard Malamud

Daniel Stern/1975

Bernard Malamud lives in a white clapboard house in Bennington, Vermont. Spacious and comfortable, it sits on a gentle downward slope, behind it the rise of the Green Mountains. To this house on April 26, 1974, came friends, family, colleagues and the children of friends—to celebrate Malamud's sixtieth birthday. It was a sunny weekend, the weather and ambience, benign, friendly.

There were about a half dozen young people taking their rest in sleeping bags in various bedrooms and in a home volunteered by a friend and neighbor. Three of them, from nearby universities, were children of friends on the faculty of Oregon State University more than a dozen years ago.

On Saturday night there was a birthday party, with champagne, birthday cake and dancing. At the end of the evening the young people drummed up a show of slides: scenes of past travels: in particular, scenes of Corvallis, Oregon, where Malamud had lived and taught for 12 years before returning East.

Bernard Malamud is a slender man with a greying mustache and inquisitive brown eyes that search and hide a little at the same time. He is a quiet man who listens a lot, and responds freely. His wife, Anne, an attractive, articulate woman of Italian descent, had planned the party, assisted by the young people from Oregon, and the Malamuds' son, Paul, and daughter, Janna.

The taping of the interview began late Friday morning, on the back porch which overlooks a long descending sweep of lawn and, in the distance, the encircling mountains. It was continued, later, in the book-filled study where Malamud writes. (He also writes in his office at Bennington College.) At first he was conscious of the tape-recorder, but grew less so as the session—and the weekend—continued. He has a quick laugh and found it easy to discourse on the questions asked. An ironic humor would seem to be his mother tongue.

Interviewer: Why sixty? I understand that when *The Paris Review* asked you to do an interview after the publication of *The Fixer* you suggested doing it when you hit sixty?

Malamud: Right. It's a respectable round number and when it becomes your age you look at it with both eyes. It's a good time to see from. In the past I sometimes resisted interviews because I had no desire to talk about myself in relation to my fiction. There are people who always want to make you a character in your stories and want you to confirm it. Of course there's some truth to it: Every character you invent takes his essence from you; therefore you're in them as Flaubert was in Emma—but, peace to him, you are not those you imagine. They are your fictions. And I don't like questions of explication: What did I mean by this or that?—I want the books to speak for themselves. You can read?—all right, tell me what my books mean. Astonish me.

Interviewer: What about a little personal history? There's been little written about your life.

Malamud: That's how I wanted it. I like privacy and as much as possible to stay out of my books. I know that's disadvantageous to certain legitimate kinds of criticism of literature, but my needs come first. Still I have here and there talked a little about my life: My father was a grocer; my mother, who helped him, after a long illness, died young. I had a younger brother who lived a hard and lonely life and died in his fifties. My mother and father were gentle, honest, kindly people, and who they were and their affection for me to some degree made up for the cultural deprivation I felt as a child. They weren't educated but their values were stable. Though my father always managed to make a living they were comparatively poor, especially in the Depression, and yet I never heard a word in praise of the buck. On the other hand, there were no books that I remember in the house, no records, music, pictures on the wall. On Sundays I listened to somebody's piano through the window. At nine I caught pneumonia and when I was convalescing my father bought me *The Book of Knowledge,* twenty volumes where there had been none. That was, considering the circumstances, an act of great generosity.

When I was in high school he bought a radio. As a kid, for entertainment I turned to the movies and dime novels. Maybe *The Natural* derives from Frank Merriwell as well as the adventures of the Brooklyn Dodgers in Ebbets Field. Anyway, my parents stayed close to the store. Once in a while, on Jewish holidays, we went visiting, or saw a Jewish play—Sholem Aleichem, Peretz, and others. My mother's brother, Charles Fidelman, and their cousin, Isidore Cashier, were in the Yiddish theatre.

Around the neighborhood the kids played Chase the White Horse, Ringolevio, Buck-Buck, punchball and one o'cat. Occasionally we stole tomatoes from the Italian dirt farmers, gypped the El to ride to Coney Island, smoked in cellars and played blackjack. I wore sneakers every summer. My education at home derived mostly from the presence and example of good, feelingful, hardworking people. They were worriers, with other faults I wasn't much conscious of until I recognized them in myself. I learned from books, in the public schools. I had some fine teachers in grammar school, Erasmus Hall High School, and later in City College, in New York I took to literature and early wanted to be a writer.

Interviewer: How early?

Malamud: At eight or nine I was writing little stories in school and feeling the glow. To anyone of my friends who'd listen I'd recapitulate at tedious length the story of the last movie I'd seen. The movies tickled my imagination. As a writer I learned from Charlie Chaplin.

Interviewer: What in particular?

Malamud: Let's say the rhythm, the snap of comedy; the reserved comic presence—that beautiful distancing; the funny with sad; the surprise of surprise.

Interviewer: Please go on about your life.

Malamud: Schools meant a lot to me, those I went to and taught at. You learn what you teach and you learn from those you teach. In 1942 I met my wife and we were married in 1945. We have two children and have lived in Oregon, Rome, Bennington, Cambridge, London, New York, and have traveled a fair amount. In sum, once I was twenty and not so young, now I'm sixty inclined on the young side.

Interviewer: Which means?

Malamud: Largely, the life of imagination, and doing pretty much what I set out to do. I made my mistakes, took my lumps, learned. I resisted my ignorance, limitations, obsessions. I'm freer than I was. I'd rather write it than talk. I love the privileges of form.

Interviewer: You've taught during the time you were a professional writer?

Malamud: Thirty-five years—

Interviewer: There are some who say teaching doesn't do the writer much good; in fact it restricts life and homogenizes experience. Isn't a writer better off on the staff of *The New Yorker,* or working for the BBC? Faulkner fed a furnace and wrote for the movies.

Malamud: Doesn't it depend on the writer? People experience similar things differently. Sometimes I've regretted the time I've given to teaching but not teaching itself. And a community of serious readers is a miraculous thing. Some of the most extraordinary people I've met were students of mine, or colleagues. Still I ought to say I teach only a single class of prose fiction, one term a year. I've taught since I was twenty-five and though I need more time for reading and writing I also want to keep on doing what I can do well and enjoy doing.

Interviewer: Do you teach literature?

Malamud: If you teach prose fiction you are teaching literature. You teach those who want to write to read fiction, even their own work, with greater understanding. Sometimes they're suprised to find out how much they've said or not said that they didn't know they had.

Interviewer: Can one, indeed, teach writing?

Malamud: You teach writers—assuming a talent. At the beginning young writers pour it out without much knowing the nature of their talent. What you try to do is hold a mirror up to their fiction so, in a sense, they can see what they're showing. Not all who come forth are fully armed. Some are gifted in narrative, some shun it. Some show a richness of metaphor, some have to dig for it. Some writers think language is all they need; they mistake it for subject matter. Some rely on whimsy. Some on gut feeling. Some of them don't make the effort to create a significant form. They do automatic writing and think they're probing themselves. The odd thing is most young writers write traditional narrative until you introduce them to the experimental writers—not for experiment's sake, but to try something for size. Let the writer attempt whatever he can. There's no telling where he will come out stronger than before. Art is in life but the realm is endless.

Interviewer: Experiment at the beginning?

Malamud: Sometimes a new technique excites a flood of fictional ideas. Some, after experimenting, realize their strength is in traditional modes. Some, after trying several things, may give up the thought of writing fiction—not a bad thing. Writing—the problems, the commitment, the effort, scares them. Some may decide to try poetry or criticism. Some turn to painting—why not? I have no kick against those who use writing, or another art, to test themselves, to find themselves. Sometimes I have to tell them their talents are thin—not to waste their lives writing third-rate fiction.

Interviewer: Fidelman as a painter? The doubtful talent?

Malamud: Yes. Among other things it is a book about finding a vocation. Forgive the soft impeachment.

Interviewer: In *Fidelman* and *The Tenants* you deal with artists who can't produce, or produce badly. Why does the subject interest you so much? Have you ever been blocked?

Malamud: Never. Even in anxiety I've written, though anxiety, because it is monochromatic, may limit effects. I like the drama of non-productivity, especially where there may be talent. It's an interesting ambiguity: the force of the creative versus the paralysis caused by the insults, the confusions of life.

Interviewer: What about work habits? Some writers, especially at the beginning, have problems settling how to do it.

Malamud: There's no one way—there's so much drivel about this subject. You're who you are, not Fitzgerald or Thomas Wolfe. You write by sitting down and writing. There's no particular time or place—you suit yourself, your nature. How one works, assuming he's disciplined, doesn't matter. If he or she is not disciplined, no sympathetic magic will help. The trick is to make time—not steal it—and produce the fiction. If the stories come, you get them written, you're on the right track. Eventually everyone learns his or her own best way. The real mystery to crack is you.

Interviewer: What about the number of drafts? Some writers write only one.

Malamud: They're cheating themselves. First drafts are for

learning what your novel or story is about. Revision is working with
that knowledge to enlarge and enhance an idea, to re-form it. D.H.
Lawrence, for instance, did seven or eight drafts of *The Rainbow*.
The first draft of a book is the most uncertain—where you need guts,
the ability to accept the imperfect until it is better. Revision is one of
the true pleasures of writing. "The men and things of today are wont
to lie fairer and truer in tomorrow's memory," Thoreau said.

Interviewer: Do you teach your own writing?

Malamud: No, I teach what I know about writing.

Interviewer: What specific piece of advice would you give to
young writers?

Malamud: Write your heart out.

Interviewer: Anything else?

Malamud: Watch out for self-deceit in fiction. Write truthfully but
with cunning.

Interviewer: Anything special to more experienced types?

Malamud: To any writer: Teach yourself to work in uncertainty.
Many writers are anxious when they begin, or try something new.
Even Matisse painted some of his fauvist pictures in anxiety. Maybe
that helped him to simplify. Character, discipline, negative capability
count. Write, complete, revise. If it doesn't work begin something
else.

Interviewer: And if it doesn't work twenty or thirty times?

Malamud: You live your life as best you can.

Interviewer: I've heard you talk about the importance of subject
matter?

Malamud: It's always a problem. Very young writers who don't
know themselves obviously often don't know what they have to say.
Sometimes by staying with it they write themselves into a fairly rich
vein. Some, by the time they find what they're capable of writing
about, no longer want to write. Some go through psychoanalysis or a
job in a paint factory and begin to write again. One hopes they then
have something worth saying. Nothing is guaranteed. Some writers
have problems with subject matter not in their first book, which may
mine childhood experience, or an obsession, or fantasy, or the story
they've carried in their minds and imagination to this point, but after
that—after this first yield—often they run into trouble with their next
few books. Especially if the first book is unfortunately a best seller.

And some writers run into difficulties at the end, particularly if they exclude important areas of personal experience from their writing. Hemingway would not touch his family beyond glimpses in short stories, mostly the Nick Adams pieces. He once wrote his brother that their mother was a bitch and father a suicide—who'd want to read about them? Obviously not all experience is available to a writer for purposes of fiction, but I feel that if Hemingway had tried during his last five years, let's say, to write about his father rather than the bulls once more, or the big fish, he mightn't have committed suicide. Mailer, after *The Naked and the Dead,* ran into trouble he couldn't resolve until he invented his mirror-image, Aquarius, Prisoner of Sex, Döppelgänger, without whom he can't write. After he had invented "Norman Mailer" he produced *The Armies of the Night,* a beautiful feat of prestidigitation, if not fiction. He has still to write, Richard Poirier says, his *Moby Dick.* To write a good big novel he will have to invent other selves, richly felt selves. Roth, since *Portnoy,* has been hunting for a fruitful subject. He's tried various strategies to defeat the obsession of the hated wife he almost never ceases to write about. He'll have at last to bury her to come up with a new comedy.

Interviewer: What about yourself?

Malamud: I say the same thing in different worlds.

Interviewer: Anything else to say to writers—basic stuff?

Malamud: Take chances. "Dare to do," Eudora Welty says. She's right. One drags around a bag of fears he has to throw to the winds every so often if he expects to take off in his writing. I'm glad Virginia Woolf did *Orlando*, though it isn't my favorite of her books, and in essence she was avoiding a subject. Still, you don't have to tell everything you know. I like Updike's *Centaur,* Bellow's *Henderson.* Genius, after it has got itself together, may give out with a *Ulysses* or *Remembrance of Things Past.* One doesn't have to imitate the devices of Joyce or Proust, but if you're not a genius imitate the daring. If you are a genius assert yourself, in art and humanity.

Interviewer: Humanity? Are you suggesting art is moral?

Malamud: It tends toward morality. It values life. Even when it doesn't it tends to. My former colleague, Stanley Edgar Hyman, used to say that even the act of creating a form is a moral act. That leaves out something, but I understand and like what he was driving at. It's close to Frost's definition of a poem as "a momentary stay against confusion." Morality begins with an awareness of the sanctity of one's life, hence the lives of others—even Hitler's to begin with—the sheer privilege of being, in this miraculous cosmos, and trying to figure out why. Art, in essence, celebrates life and gives us our measure.

Interviewer: It changes the world?

Malamud: It changes me. It affirms me.

Interviewer: Really?

Malamud: (*laughs*) It helps.

Interviewer: Let's get to your books. In *The Natural*, why the baseball-mythology combination?

Malamud: Baseball flat is baseball flat. I had to do something else to enrich the subject. I love metaphor. It provides two loaves where there seems to be one. Sometimes it throws in a load of fish. The mythological analogy is a system of metaphor. It enriches the vision without resorting to montage. This guy gets up with his baseball bat and all at once he is, through the ages, a knight—somewhat battered—with a lance; not to mention a guy with a blackjack, or someone attempting murder with a flower. You relate to the past and predict the future. I'm not talented as a conceptual thinker but I am in the uses of metaphor. The mythological and symbolic excite my imagination. Incidentally, Keats said: "I am not a conceptual thinker, I am a man of ideas."

Interviewer: Is *The Assistant* mythological?

Malamud: Some, I understand, find it so.

Interviewer: Did you set it up as a mythology?

Malamud: No. If it's mythological to some readers I have no objection. You read the book and write your ticket. I can't tell you how the words fall, though I know what I mean. Your interpretation—*pace*, S. Sontag—may enrich the book or denude it. All I ask is that it be consistent and make sense.

Interviewer: Is it a moral allegory?

Malamud: You have to squeeze your brain to come up with that. The spirit is more than moral and by the same token there's more than morality in a good man. One must make room in those he creates. So far as range is concerned, ultimately a writer's mind and heart, if any, are revealed in his fiction.

Interviewer: What is the source of *The Assistant*?

Malamud: Source questions are piddling but you're my friend so

I'll tell you. Mostly my father's life as a grocer, though not necessarily my father. Plus three short stories, sort of annealed in a single narrative: "The Cost of Living" and "The First Seven Years"—both in *The Magic Barrel*. And a story I wrote in the forties, "The Place is Different Now," which I've not included in my story collections.

Interviewer: Is *The Fixer* also related to your father's life?

Malamud: Indirectly. My father told me the Mendel Beilis story when I was a kid. I carried it around almost forty years and decided to use it after I gave up the idea of a Sacco and Vanzetti novel. When I began to read for the Sacco and Vanzetti it had all the quality of a structured fiction, all the necessary elements of theme and narrative. I couldn't see any way of re-forming it. I was very much interested in the idea of prison as a source of the self's freedom and thought of Dreyfus next, but he was a dullish man, and though he endured well he did not suffer well. Neither did Beilis for that matter but his drama was more interesting—his experiences; so I invented Yakov Bok, with perhaps the thought of him as a potential Vanzetti. Beilis, incidentally, died a bitter man, in New York—after leaving Palestine, because he thought he hadn't been adequately reimbursed for his suffering.

Interviewer: Some critics have commented on this prison motif in your work.

Malamud: Perhaps I use it as a metaphor for the dilemma of all men: necessity, whose bars we look through and try not to see. Social injustice, apathy, ignorance. The personal prison of entrapment in past experience, guilt, obsession—the somewhat blind or blinded self, in other words. A man has to construct, invent, his freedom. Imagination helps. A truly great man or woman extends it for others in the process of creating his/her own.

Interviewer: Does this idea or theme, as you call it, come out of your experience as a Jew?

Malamud: That's probably in it—a heightened sense of prisoner of history, but there's more to it than that. I conceive this as the major battle in life, to transcend the self—extend one's realm of freedom.

Interviewer: Not all your characters do.

Malamud: Obviously. But they're all more or less engaged in the enterprise.

Interviewer: Humor is so much a part of your work. Is this an easy quality to deal with? Is one problem that the response to humor is so much a question of individual taste?

Malamud: The funny bone is universal. I doubt humorists think of individual taste when they're enticing the laugh. With me humor comes unexpectedly, usually in defense of a character, sometimes because I need cheering up. When something starts funny I can feel my imagination eating and running. I love the distancing—the guise of invention—that humor gives fiction. Comedy, I imagine, is harder to do consistently than tragedy, but I like it spiced in the wine of sadness.

Interviewer: What about suffering? It's a subject much in your early work.

Malamud: I'm against it but when it occurs why waste the experience?

Interviewer: Are you a Jewish writer?

Malamud: What is the question asking?

Interviewer: One hears various definitions and insistences, for instance, that one is primarily a writer and any subject matter is secondary; or that one is an American-Jewish writer. There are qualifications, by Bellow, Roth, others.

Malamud: I'm an American, I'm a Jew, and I write for all men. A novelist has to or he's built himself a cage. I write about Jews, when I write about Jews, because they set my imagination going. I know something about their history, the quality of their experience and belief, and of their literature, though not as much as I would like. Like many writers I'm influenced especially by the Bible, both Testaments. I respond in particular to the East European immigrants of my father's and mother's generation; many of them were Jews of the Pale as described by the classic Yiddish writers. And of course I've been deeply moved by the Jews of the concentration camps, and the refugees wandering from nowhere to nowhere. I'm concerned about Israel. Nevertheless, Jews like Rabbis Kahane and Korrf set my teeth on edge. Sometimes I make characters Jewish because I think I will understand them better as people, not because I am out to prove anything. That's a qualification. Still another is that I know that, as a writer, I've been influenced by Hawthorne, James, Mark Twain, Hemingway, more than I have been by Sholem Aleichem and I.L. Peretz, whom I read with pleasure. Of course I admire and have been moved by other writers, Dostoyevsky and Chekhov, for instance, but the point I'm making is that I was born in America and respond, in American life, to more than Jewish experience. I wrote for those who read.

Interviewer: Thus S. Levin is Jewish and not much is made of it?

Malamud: He was a gent who interested me in a place that interested me. He was out to be educated.

Interviewer: Occasionally I see a remark to the effect that he has more than a spoonful of you in him.

Malamud: So have Roy Hobbs, Helen Bober, Willie Spearmint and Talking Horse. More to the point—I prefer autobiographical essence to autobiographical history. Events from life may creep into the narrative but it isn't necessarily my life history.

Interviewer: How much of a book is set in your mind when you begin? Do you begin at the beginning? Does its course ever change markedly from what you had in the original concept?

Malamud: When I start I have a pretty well developed idea what the book is about and how it ought to go, because generally I've been thinking about it and making notes for months if not years. Generally I have the ending in mind, usually the last paragraph almost verbatim. I begin at the beginning and stay close to the track, if it is a track and not a whalepath. If it turns out I'm in the open sea, my compass is my narrative instinct, with an assist by that astrolabe, theme. The destination, wherever it is, is, as I said, already defined. If I go astray it's not a long excursis, good for getting to know the ocean if not the world. The original idea, altered but recognizable, on the whole remains.

Interviewer: Do characters ever run away from you and take on identities you hadn't expected?

Malamud: My characters run away but not far. Their guise is surprises.

Interviewer: Let's go to Fidelman. You seem to like to write about painters?

Malamud: I know a few. I love painting.

Interviewer: Rembrandt and who else?

Malamud: Too many to name, but Cezanne, Monet, and Matisse, very much, among Modernists.

Interviewer: Chagall?

Malamud: Not that much. He rides his nostalgic nag to death.

Interviewer: Some have called you a Chagallean writer.

Malamud: Their problem. I used Chagallean imagery intentionally in one story, "The Magic Barrel," and that's it. My quality is not much like his.

Interviewer: Fidelman first appears in "The Last Mohican," a short story. Did you already have in mind that there would be an extended work on him?

Malamud: After I wrote the story in Rome I jotted down ideas for several incidents in the form of a picaresque novel. I was out to loosen up—experiment a little—with narrative structure. And I wanted to see, if I wrote it at intervals—as I did from 1957 to 1968—whether the passing of time and mores would influence his life. I did not think of the narrative as merely a series of related stories because almost at once I had the structure of a novel in mind and each part had to fit that form. Robert Scholes in *The Saturday Review* has best explained what I was up to in Fidelman.

Interviewer: Did you use all the incidents you jotted down?

Malamud: No.

Interviewer: Can you give me an example of one you left out?

Malamud: Yes, Fidelman administering to the dying Keats in Rome—doing Severn's job, one of the few times in his life our boy is engaged in a purely unselfish act, or acts. But I felt I had no need to predict a change in him, especially in a sort of dream sequence, so I dropped the idea. The painting element was to come in via some feverish watercolors of John Keats, dying.

Interviewer: Fidelman is characterized by some critics as a schlemiel.

Malamud: Not accurately. Peter Schlemiel lost his shadow and suffered the consequences for all time. Not Fidelman. He does better. He escapes his worst fate. I dislike the schlemiel characterization as a taxonomical device. I said somewhere that it reduces to stereotypes people of complex motivations and fates. One can often behave like a schlemiel without being one.

Interviewer: Do you read criticism of your work?

Malamud: When it hits me in the eye, even some reviews.

Interviewer: Does it affect you?

Malamud: Some of it must. Not the crap, the self-serving pieces, but an occasional insightful criticism, favorable or unfavorable, that confirms my judgment of my work. While I'm on the subject, I dislike particularly those critics who preach their esthetic or ideological doctrines at you. What's important to them is not what the writer has done but how it fits, or doesn't fit, the thesis they want to develop. Nobody can tell a writer what can or ought to be done, or not done, in his fiction. A living death if you fall for it.

Interviewer: That narration, for instance, is dead or dying?

Malamud: It'll be dead when the penis is.

Interviewer: What about the death of the novel?

Malamud: The novel could disappear but it won't die.

Interviewer: How does that go?

Malamud: I'm not saying it will disappear, just entertaining the idea. Assume it does; then someday a talented writer writes himself a long heartfelt letter and the form reappears. The human race needs the novel. We need all the experience we can get. Those who say the novel is dead can't write them.

Interviewer: You've done two short stories and a novel about blacks. Where do you get your material?

Malamud: Experience and books. I lived on the edge of a black neighborhood in Brooklyn when I was a boy. I played with blacks in the Flatbush Boys Club. I had a friend—Buster; we used to go to his house every so often. I swiped dimes so we could go to the movies together on a couple of Saturday afternoons. After I was married I taught for a year in a black evening high school in Harlem. The short stories derive from that period. I also read black fiction and history.

Interviewer: What set off *The Tenants*?

Malamud: Jews and blacks, the period of the troubles in New York City; the teachers strike, the rise of black activism, the mix-up of cause and effect. I thought I'd say a word.

Interviewer: Why the three endings?

Malamud: Because one wouldn't do.

Interviewer: Will you predict how it will be between blacks and Jews in the future?

Malamud: How can one? All I know is that American blacks have been badly treated. We, as a society, have to redress the balance. Those who want for others must expect to give up something. What we get in return is the affirmation of what we believe in.

Interviewer: You give a sense in your fiction that you try not to repeat yourself?

Malamud: Good. In my books I go along the same paths in different worlds.

Interviewer: What's the path—theme?

Malamud: Derived from one's sense of values, it's a vision of life, a feeling for people—real qualities in imaginary worlds.

Interviewer: Do you like writing short stories more than you do novels?

Malamud: Just as much, though the short story has its own pleasures. I like packing a self or two into a few pages, predicating lifetimes. The drama is terse, happens faster, and is often outlandish. A short story is a way of indicating the complexity of life in a few pages, producing the surprise and effect of a profound knowledge in a short time. There's, among other things, a drama, a resonance, of the reconciliation of opposites: much to say, a little time to say it, something like the effect of a poem.

Interviewer: You write them between novels?

Malamud: Yes, to breathe, and give myself time to think what's in the next book. Sometimes I'll try out a character or situation similar to that in a new novel.

Interviewer: How many drafts do you usually do of a novel?

Malamud: Many more than I call three. Usually the last of the first puts it in place. The second focuses, develops, subtilizes. By the third most of the dross is gone. I work with language. I love the flowers of afterthought.

Interviewer: Your style has always seemed so individual, so recognizable. Is this a natural gift, or is it contrived and honed?

Malamud: My style flows from the fingers. The eye and ear approve or amend.

Interviewer: Let's wind up. Are you optimistic about the future?

Malamud: My nature is optimistic but not the evidence—population misery, famine, politics of desperation, the prolifer-ation of the atom bomb. Mylai, one minute after Hiroshima in history, was ordained. We're going through long, involved, trans-formations of world society, ongoing upheavals of colonialism, old modes of distribution, mores, overthrowing the slave mentality. With luck we may end up in a society with a larger share of the world's goods, opportunities for education, freedom, going to the presently underprivileged. Without luck there may be a vast economic redistribution without political freedom. In the Soviet Union, as it is presently constituted, that's meant the kiss of death to freedom in art and literature. I worry that democracy which has protected us from this indignity, especially in the United States, suffers from a terrifying inadequacy of leadership, and the apathy, unimaginativeness, and hard-core selfishness of too many of us. I worry about technology rampant. I fear those who are by nature beastly.

Interviewer: What does one write novels about nowadays?

Malamud: Whatever wants to be written.

Interviewer: Is there something I haven't asked you that you might want to comment on?

Malamud: No.

Interviewer: For instance, what writing has meant to you?

Malamud: I'd be too moved to say.

Bernard Malamud—An Interview

E.H. Leelavathi Masilamoni/1976

From the *Indian Journal of American Studies*, 9 (1979), 33-37.
Reprinted by permission.

E.H. Leelavathi Masilamoni is a lecturer at Osmania University, Hyderabad. In 1975–76 she was a Fulbright Scholar at the University of Denver and the State University of New York at Buffalo. She interviewed Malamud in his study in Bennington, Vermont, on 1 June 1976.

Interviewer: Do you feel an outsider in America?

Malamud: No. On the contrary, I feel an insider. In fact, feeling an insider is partly an imaginative act, because I couldn't write as an American if I didn't feel an insider.

Interviewer: What do you think are the important characteristics of writing?

Malamud: One is the ability to tell a story, the other is the ability to penetrate the human self, based on an understanding and realization of character. I feel that character is primary to the novel, rather than plot, because mysterious elements of human life and society are invisible and can't be defined unless described.

Interviewer: What have you to say about the future of the novel?

Malamud: I think it is healthy, and marvellous for portraying various kinds of human drama. There will be writers and writers and there will be a genius.

Interviewer: Is there a genius now?

Malamud: No, there is no genius now, but obviously there has been in the recent past. Proust, Joyce, and D. H. Lawrence have all displayed genius.

Interviewer: English literature is more American than English. Have you any comments to make?

Malamud: English writing is English writing. They have been influenced by American writing but it would be impossible to say that they are more American than English.

Interviewer: What do you think of popular literature?

Malamud: Whom do you mean? Writers like Harold Robbins and others?

Interviewer: Yes.

Malamud: I don't think it is important because fictionally, intellectually, spiritually and imaginatively, what they write is thin. I feel this even though in terms of numbers their reading public is very large.

Interviewer: What do you think of *Humboldt's Gift?*

Malamud: I like it though I don't think it is Bellow's best book. I find my name very often coupled with his, but I can never write as he does. His books are idea-centred, mine are people-centred. I enjoy reading his books and I think he is very good.

Interviewer: Novelists have shown concern over assimilation and survival. What is your concern?

Malamud: Survival, of course! I am deeply aware of World War II and the horrors of the concentration camps. It is a personal thing and I have been, to some degree, conditioned by this experience. Any sensitive human being who calls himself Jewish could not ignore the holocaust.

Interviewer: This, I believe, has influenced your writing—especially the short stories.

Malamud: To some degree. I write about the marginal Jew who manages to be influenced by the concepts of morality which, incidentally, are Jewish but not only Jewish.

Interviewer: I am using a quotation from Leslie Fiedler—

Malamud: Go ahead.

Interviewer: "One of the problems of the practicing Jewish-American novelist arises from his need to create his protagonists not only out of the life he knows, but against the literature on which he and his readers have been nurtured." Is this true of you?

Malamud: That's every novelist's problem. My problem is how to invent a human being. Whether he is Jewish or not is not important. I want to create a character who lives.

Interviewer: For whom do you write?

Malamud: I write for anyone who can read. I write for Indians, Japanese, Hungarians, British—anyone who can read.

Interviewer: Your works deal with the possibilities of man, and are concerned with love. I find that from *The Natural* to *The Fixer,* there is a demonstration of faith in the possibilities of man. In *The Natural*, erotic love is a way of self-transcendence and even though Roy Hobbs is a failure, there is a faint glimmer of hope towards the end.

Malamud: Yes. Love starts with egoism but everyone can't give love. Only the mature man or woman can do it.

Interviewer: In *The Assistant*, Frank Alpine is more successful. He moves towards self-transcendence, but elements of selfishness are still present. He works to help Helen realize her ambitions in the hope of winning her.

Malamud: Yes.

Interviewer: In *A New Life* there is further development. S. Levin accepts responsibility for Pauline and her kids even though he ceases to love her.

Malamud: No! I don't agree. Levin has not ceased to love her. There can be no responsibility without some love. The golden hoop rings he gave her which she fastened on to her ears are a symbol of love, to me symbolic of the wedding ring.

Interviewer: Well, maybe my reading of it is wrong.

Malamud: Many feel this way. But it is not true. I haven't read the book since I wrote it. I never read my books once I've finished writing them. But I am sure he still loves her.

Interviewer: Yes, there is love, but it is a different type of love. It is no longer selfish; he could have walked out on her but he didn't, at the expense of his career.

Malamud: Yes, of course.

Interviewer: The fixer, most certainly, is your complete hero. He demonstrates agapean love in his acceptance of Raisl's son as his own and in not pleading guilty. He bears his ordeal rather than plead guilty because he thinks of the entire Jewish community. Until *The Fixer* your books demonstrate a faith in man. But with *The Tenants*, I see a change. The protagonists fail to demonstrate love.

Malamud: Well, there are three endings and that is one. There is an ending in a wedding.

Interviewer: There is a clear indication of loss of faith in man. Am I right? Why has this happened?

Malamud: Yes. My faith in humanity has been bruised to some degree.

Interviewer: This is very evident in the novel.

Malamud: I am glad I have made my point.

Interviewer: Regarding love in the flesh, do you consider it baser or of a lower nature?

Malamud: Are you asking me to place love in a certain type of order?

Interviewer: Yes.

Malamud: Man must consider love a gift in life. A gift of nature which he must use as a gift. The wisest man will consider it a gift. It is a pleasure in itself but it should induce a love of life—yours, mine. Pure sexuality, sheer pleasure of living life is an enjoyment. There should be an awareness of creativity, and indulgence in the act of creation. But there is another aspect also. Love in essence enlarges the self and compels the self to ask "What does it mean? What should it mean?" Man must be his full self without deprecating the physical quality of love. One can discover oneself through physical love. It should lead to self-knowledge—knowing. Do you get what I mean?

Interviewer: Yes. But don't you think this is difficult?

Malamud: Yes, love is difficult. In a special sense it is difficult to attain. Find and give what you can in love. The future of a human being is less if love means just sleeping around. Love is something more. It comes back to the definition of life. What is life—these 60 to 70 years we have? What can we do with it if we do not love?

Interviewer: The Jew, as imagined by you, has a moral responsibility towards his brother. This emphasis makes it almost vital, at times, that he suppress some of his natural drives. Isn't this idealistic?

Malamud: Yes, but one must accept limits on one's needs in order to live effectively with others, so that the gift of life may function.

Interviewer: I hope I am not asking the wrong question.

Malamud: There is no wrong question.

Interviewer: Much of what you write testifies to Jewishness and yet I find a strong element of Christianity also. Am I right?

Malamud: Recently I met an Argentinian who said he read my books as those of an American writer. My Hungarian publisher also said the same thing. The heart doesn't have a single religion. It goes where the heart is. I have been influenced by Buddha, Jesus, and Francis of Assissi, as you see in *The Assistant.* Christianity as a theology does not interest me, but what is brought out in Christianity as a result of Jesus and St. Francis as men. I appreciate their response to human beings and the elements of nature (St. Francis responded to animals and birds). Any stimuli can be a force for the rest of a human being's life. I read the New Testament and found it stirred deep feelings in me.

Interviewer: Regarding your attitude to nature—

Malamud: There is very little of it—

Interviewer: Yes, but there is nature in *The Natural* and—

Malamud: Yes, go on.

Interviewer: I find that your attitude to nature is like that of Hardy.

Malamud: Not exactly, though I love Hardy. I am now reading a book, *Young Thomas Hardy* by Robert Gittings.

Interviewer: I think you go beyond Hardy.

Malamud: No! No! No! Hardy is a great writer.

Interviewer: You are optimistic, while Hardy is pessimistic.

Malamud: Hardy is a great writer. Yes, the element of coincidence is overused in his novels. It is interesting you ask me this question now. I am working on my next novel which has much to do with nature. It also deals with middle age, marriage and children. It will take about three years to come out.

Interview: Bernard Malamud

Mary Long/1976

From *Mademoiselle*, 82 (August, 1976), 235. Copyright © 1976 by The Condé Nast Publications Inc. Reprinted by permission.

Here is a frail bird of a man, sitting in his study, saying some wise and ingenuous things in a voice a little weighted with age. His audience is young, hushed, slightly soft-eyed. He is a storyteller, you see, and his art is always there, always that beauty and tenderness in the telling.

This is Bernard Malamud, best known as the brilliant novelist whose books win all the prizes. Today, however, he is just a kind and very intelligent man who believes he has some advice to give because you are young and interested in writing; the sort of man you can't help but like immediately.

For one thing, like his unfashionable fictional heroes, he possesses the kind of resonance that comes from a sense that there is wisdom or meaning that stretches a good way beneath the surface. And, blessedly, he does not fit the cliché about writers that says that their books are generally more interesting than they are. Malamud's learned a good deal about writing in the 60-odd years he's been working at it, a fact he does not hesitate to mention. And when he has a group of young writers in his grasp he gives his advice with church-deacon candor.

"There are enormously talented people around but the problem is getting organized to use your talents. A lot of people lose it," he warned us, "they just lose it. Life starts turning somersaults over your back and the next thing you know you're confronting things that seem to you more important than getting organized to do your writing. And if you can't get organized, then you can kiss your talent goodbye. It happens in so many cases, it's almost a loss, as though you had a field of flowers and were never able to collect them."

Malamud will tell you quite frankly that if his life is filled with flowers now, it is only because he is a strongly disciplined man willing to pace his life so that work is produced.

And it's narration, telling a story, explaining, teaching, that is most clearly connected with his own journey, his own seeking of life. "Narrative tries to find the way from one condition into another more blessed."

Now, just when you are thinking this aura of other-worldness is suspect, Malamud hands you a razor-sharp pin of practicality honed from his own bouts of self-analysis.

"I just want to show you you're not locked in any one way. You must try everything. You can try and really flop on your face—there's no question. Okay, so you flop on your face—and if you don't have enough comedy in you to enjoy the sight of yourself flopping on your face, then you're limited. Anything that moves you is worthy of fiction. Anything."

Author of *A New Life* Likes Coming Back

John Marshall/1977

From The Gazette-Times, Corvallis, Oregon, 5 May 1977. Reprinted by permission.

In his novel, the town was Easchester and the school was Cascadia College—fictional places in a work of fiction. But those in Corvallis recognized much they were familiar with when Bernard Malamud published *A New Life* in 1961.

That was no big surprise. Malamud had taught in the English department at Oregon State College from 1949 until 1961 and it was widely known that he was writing a book loosely based on his experiences here.

Publication of the book prompted a furious guessing game which preoccupied Corvallis for some time. Who was Pauline, the faculty wife who had an affair with protagonist S. Levin? Where was the barn where Levin took a waitress he had picked up in a downtown tavern? Who was Duffy, the ousted radical in the English department?

That such questions are still asked today—over 15 years after *A New Life* was published—brings a smile of amusement to the kindly face of Malamud. He is visiting Corvallis this week to renew acquaintances and give a reading of his new work at 8 p.m. tonight in Milam Auditorium.

It is Malamud's fourth trip back to the town he transformed into the fictional Easchester. And in an interview Wednesday, he said he is glad to be back.

Malamud was rhapsodic about springtime in Corvallis.

"This is a joyous coming for me," he said. "In the spring, you get a real sense of the beauty of this place—the huge clouds and the extraordinary greenery. There are just so many different varieties of green."

Malamud, however, was much less enthusiastic about how much Corvallis had grown and how much more it's expected to grow in the next few years.

76

He said, "I can't say I'm happy to see the way houses are now clustered in what seemed to have been a great amount of land to me years ago."

But he also saw change for the better in Corvallis. He said that 2nd Street today reminds him of what 3rd Street was like when he lived here. And he called the development of a place like the Old World Center, a group of specialty shops with a concert area in downtown Corvallis, "a thing you never could have forseen for Corvallis."

Talking of buildings but perhaps hinting at more, Malamud summarized, "Corvallis' architecture was bland and conservative when I was here. Now, there's really a much larger sense of the new."

Malamud also marvels at the development of OSU, which he says offers much broader opportunities for study in the humanities under a more varied faculty than when he was here.

"OSU now has a place as an important educational institution— one that easily competes with what's offered in Eugene," he said.

Malamud's fondness for Corvallis is fast evident and probably shouldn't be surprising. After all, much of Malamud's rise to a writer of national reputation took place when he lived here. He makes a particular effort to deny any rumors which may persist that he was as unhappy here as was Levin, the protagonist in *A New Life*.

"People who try to create the legend that being in Corvallis was an unhappy time for me are absolutely wrong," he said. "My bitterness toward Corvallis just doesn't exist; if it did, I wouldn't come back."

Differentiating between himself and the character of Levin is a game which Malamud is obviously weary of playing. Certain similarities are indeed evident—both are New Yorkers who left the East to teach at small colleges in the Northwest, for example. But unlike Levin, Malamud was not a bachelor who lived in a rooming house; he, in fact, was married and had two children while living here. And he didn't leave in disgrace after just one year of teaching.

What Malamud is far more willing to discuss about *A New Life* is how it illustrates the way a fiction writer draws on his own experiences to create his world of fiction.

Malamud stressed, "Fiction is not biography even though you take from biography. When people ask if my work is autobiographical, I make the point that I'm not interested in autobiography. What I'm interested in is taking qualities and essences from my experiences and then inventing fiction around them.

"People are wrong who think that I'm writing a history of what happened to me. I am an inventive writer and I'm also a fantasist.

"If people are going to make S. Levin out of me, they're also going to have to make Roy Hobbs and the Fixer and all my other protagonists out of me. If I'm one of them, I'm all of them."

To prove his point, Malamud mentioned that after publication of *The Natural*—his novel about baseball player Hobbs—he was asked to write about baseball spring training for a national magazine. He turned down the offer because he says he simply wasn't qualified to write about real baseball.

"My knowledge of baseball is solely derived from watching the Dodgers in Ebbetts Field when I was a boy," he said.

Malamud also explained why he chose to turn Corvallis into Easchester (a word play on the town name of Westchester), Oregon State College into Cascadia College and the Willamette into the Sacajawea in *A New Life*. He said he was following a well-established tradition in literature to fictionalize place names.

"You make the places an abstraction so that people can move easily into the fiction," he said. "It takes you from the rooted place where you are and sets you flying."

Malamud laughed when asked the whimsical question of what happened to Levin and Pauline, the two main characters of *A New Life*, after the end of the book. In the novel, they are last seen heading for San Francisco and probable married life together.

"I honestly don't know what happens to them," said the author. "All I can do is bring them to the last page; what they do after that is their business."

But although the question was not asked seriously, Malamud went on to say that it pointed to something he hoped to accomplish with his work.

"For the reader to wonder what could have happened to the characters after finishing the book is exactly what the writer of fiction wants you to do," he said.

Malamud, 63, has won the National Book Award for *The Magic Barrel,* as well as both the Pulitzer Prize and the National Book Award for *The Fixer*. But he remains a quiet-spoken man who still retains an obvious dislike for the public demands of being one of the country's best known writers.

"I'm happy to have the awards which my fiction has won for itself, but I don't want them interfering with my life.

"I find it (fame) inconvenient. It interferes with my privacy. I happen to be the kind of person who likes to meet people on a human level; I like them to be able to make up their own minds about me."

Malamud is now a faculty member at Bennington College in Bennington, Vt. But he teaches only one course each spring and devotes most of his time to writing.

He has recently entered the fifth year of work on his next novel which is entitled *Dubin's Lives*. It is the story of a middle-aged biographer whose study of the life of D.H. Lawrence leads him to try to both understand and experiment with his own life. One chapter of the new book was published in the April 18 and 25 issues of *The New Yorker*, but final publication of the whole work is not expected before the end of 1978.

Malamud's writing regimen on the book usually involves writing from about 9 a.m. to 1 p.m. every day except Sunday. He works in his study—interrupted by several visits each morning from his wife.

Malamud writes in long hand, then retypes his final drafts.

"I think it's easier to pursue a thought with a pen; you can think more clearly between words," he said. "In handwriting, words don't seem as sacred as they do when they're typed up."

A Talk with the Novelist

Ralph Tyler/1979

From *The New York Times Book Review*, 18 February, 1979 1, 31-34. Copyright © 1979 by The New York Times Company. Reprinted by permission.

"My morale is dancing at the moment," Bernard Malamud said on the eve of the publication of *Dubin's Lives*, a novel that took five and half years of his life. Although the reviewers the public reads had not yet returned their verdicts, Farrar, Straus & Giroux, Malamud's publishers, were confident enough to schedule a generous first printing of 50,000 copies. Mr. Malamud was not pretending to be blasé about these early signs of favor. "When you work as hard as I did," he said, "you want that particular payoff."

Appropriately, it was snowing in New York when the author was interviewed at his West Side apartment about a novel that is much preoccupied with the seasons of both nature and man, particularly the ravages of winter. Mr. Malamud, 64, who spends most of the year in Vermont, where he teaches one term a year at Bennington College, has been sheltering each winter for the last 10 in his native New York. By the time the book came out, he and his wife of 33 years, Ann, planned to be in milder Capri, where friends had lent them a villa for three weeks. He said he would use his Italian stay to prepare for his spring semester's course at Bennington—on Virginia Woolf—and to decide what there is for him still to write in the short story (three collections have been published) and the novel (*Dubin* is his seventh).

Mr. Malamud has been known to be reluctant about interviews, but he says that this is a thing of the past, when "I was often disappointed by people talking to me about work they hadn't bothered to read. And I hadn't really organized myself for interviews. Now I can handle them with greater ease. A certain kind of openness to life has developed during the course of my life that makes me more hospitable, more friendly to strangers on the doorstep."

Dressed in gray flannel trousers and a muted green sweater, Mr.

Malamud was indeed open and welcoming—but not casual. He chose his words with care, sometimes editing as he went along ("Where I said I had become more flexible, could you change that to more relaxed?"). His hair has thinned, his sideburns and mustache are white, but his five-foot, eight-inch frame has been kept within the bounds of youthful maturity. Like his hero Dubin, he loves to walk, and he does daily calisthenics to ease back pains probably caused by spending long hours bent over a desk. His eyes have the hue and intensity of polished mahogany and seem to be reading his questioner.

He said *Dubin's Lives* was his attempt at bigness, at summing up what he has learned over the long haul. "I was already approaching 60 when I began it and I had to be very severe with myself," he said. "What had my experience totaled up to? What did I know up to this point? I wanted to write a novel that was significant to me." He spent two years more than he usually does on this book and kept a journal while he was working on it—random reflections, which he intends to destroy now that they have served their purpose of self-discovery. A few sentences from the journal offer provocative glimpses:

"One must transcend the autobiographical detail by inventing it after it is remembered."

"I get the impression I am working with pieces of mosaic to create the impression of a raging river in flood."

"If it is winter in the book, spring surprises me when I look up."

That this novel is intimately connected to him, nerve end to nerve end, is clear, but Mr. Malamud insists it is not basically autobiographical. "Dubin is fictive," he said, "I am an inventor of characters. I like to be in a position to change anything I want." He also said the novel was not about middle age, as had been suggested, but about "a man's crisis during a period of three years. I am writing about one human being, not all human beings. To say it is about the whole of middle age is ridiculous. From the time below 56 you can see Dubin had a positive kind of life. He came to his middle-age crisis comparatively late and it was particularly intense."

Why had he made Dubin a biographer? Mr. Malamud said he had tried him as a cellist, "but I couldn't handle the cello, even though my son used to play it. I was aware that cello-playing was something I didn't have. What do I have? I thought of making him an artist, but I had already done that with Fidelman [the hero of his 1969 *Pictures of Fidelman*]. Then I lucked into making him a biographer. I discovered I could use the stuff and material of biography for its many sources of harmony and counterpoint."

Mr. Malamud was reluctant at first to say how the new novel differed from his earlier works. "I want the book in the book-stores," he said, "so that the public can read it and tell me. I don't like authors to establish the meaning of their books. Then you're placed in the role of making *obiter dicta,* and everybody goes around quoting the author on his book."

"But I'll take a stab at it," he continued. "The texture of it, the depth of it, the quality of human experience in it is greater than in my previous books. It is often that of the 19th-century novel. I wanted to get that quality of richness into it. But you can't write a 19th-century novel simply by wishing to. I'm a great fan of Thomas Hardy and George Eliot; I like the texture of human beings, the mystery of human life in their novels. But I want to accomplish what they did with 20th-century techniques. They would never think of using biography. I tend to work close to life with as much of a technical assist as I can get. The technique of making Dubin a biographer opens up his life, makes him more interesting and more complex."

Mr. Malamud said he chose D.H. Lawrence as Dubin's subject "because Lawrence's theories about the significant relationship of sexual experience to the deeper sources of life and beyond into a kind of mystical universe gave Dubin things he could think about more than mere experience itself. Just as in *The Natural* [Mr. Malamud's first novel, 1952] I dealt with the mythical world in order to give baseball the kind of excitement and symbolic interest I wanted, so Lawrence's theories give the world of sex a kind of deepening."

Mr. Malamud had read only one or two books by Lawrence when he started *Dubin's Lives,* but since then he has read everything. "If I ever knew a writer," he said, "I knew *him.*" His opinion of Lawrence is higher now than at the start, despite his continued distaste for what he calls "his more hateful opinions: of mass man and Jews, his blood theory."

"I felt more respect for him after I got the feeling of the whole man," he said, "particularly after a wonderful visit last spring to his home in Eastwood. He was a very generous man and very honest. He didn't lie to himself about his work. He tried to make the best of several bad situations during his life. He did a lot with his relationship to Frieda and his marriage. His letters are marvelous—among the best we have, with Keats and possibly Virginia Woolf and one or two others. All his letters are confessional. They teach you something of being forthright about life."

The other writer Dubin is closely involved with is Thoreau, whose biography he writes before beginning Lawrence's. "I had Dubin in the country," Mr. Malamud said, "and I was eager to handle nature seriously. In familiarizing myself with the writings of Thoreau I had the opportunity to reflect about nature." A feeling for the countryside has been ingrained in Mr. Malamud by the 29 years he has taught in rural settings—17 at Bennington and 12 before that at Corvallis, Ore., where he taught at Oregon State College, now Oregon State University. The Malamud's had moved from their Greenwich Village apartment shortly after the birth of Paul, their first child, to get out of the city and to live nearer Mrs. Malamud's mother in California. Although it wasn't delight in nature that took him to the job, but a step up from the evening high-school English classes he had been teaching in Brooklyn and in Harlem, the result was an intense period of nature observation.

Mr. Malamud, Brooklyn-raised, is amused that he continued to be thought of as the archetypal city writer after having lived in the country, and he is clearly pleased that he was able to bring off the many passages of nature writing in his new novel. "That was one of the little surprises I enjoyed producing. A good writer has to seek more than obvious subject matter and has to do more than repeat himself. The refreshment of a new theme is needed to set the imagination going."

Dubin's Lives is dedicated to Max and Bertha Malamud, the author's parents, and to Anna Fidelman, the widow of an uncle (he was an actor in the Second Avenue Yiddish theater). Asked what his parents were like, Malamud at first replied that this was too complex to deal with, but after a long pause said they were "simple, feelingful, troubled, human." Although he had dedicated *The Natural* to his father, a storekeeper, this was the first time he had dedicated a book to his mother, who died at 44 when Malamud was only 15. "I think she would understand this book," he said. "She also had some kind of unhappiness of middle age."

Yiddish was spoken in the home when Mr. Malamud was a child, and he said he understood it now but didn't speak it too well, although "if a poor old lady asks me directions in Yiddish I can usually answer her." In his view, some people have overemphasized the impact of Yiddish on his prose. "What I actually do best is what I would call immigrant English." He concedes, however, that he salts his dialogue with idioms that have the quality of Yiddish. As for his word order, which sometimes varies from the traditional, he said that this anomaly might derive as much from Latin or German as from Yiddish. And he believes it is to Hemingway more than Yiddish that he owes his ability to compress.

Swift transitions—changing a scene in one sentence between paragraphs—also are among the talents he prizes and something he thinks he may have learned from intercutting in motion pictures. "I was influenced very much by Charlie Chaplin's movies," he said, "by the rhythm and snap of his comedy and his wonderful, wonderful mixture of comedy and sadness—one of his major gifts that I've studied with great care."

He is not, he said, an "aficionado" of the movies made from his own books, although he thought Alan Bates "quite good" in the 1968 film of his Pulitzer Prize-winning novel, *The Fixer.* He also said he was not interested in writing for the screen "because you are not in control of the fate of the pieces of writing you do." He recalled that when Dalton Trumbo, who wrote the screenplay of *The Fixer,* sent in his draft, "I asked why didn't you leave in any of the interesting dialogue, and he said they didn't want to make Yakov [the wrongly imprisoned hero] sound too Jewish."

In the new novel Dubin is a Jew, his wife and stepson are not, and his daughter, although raised vaguely as a Jew, drifts into Zen. The young woman in his life, Fanny Bick, sometimes wears a Jewish star on a chain at her neck and sometimes a crucifix. Did Mr. Malamud, as he has so often been asked over the years, along with Saul Bellow and Philip Roth, consider himself a Jewish writer? "Jewishness is important to me, but I don't consider myself only a Jewish writer," he replied. "I have interests beyond that, and I feel I'm writing for all men."

Fanny Bick seems to reflect the modern woman's search for identity. Mr. Malamud said he had been influenced by the women's movement through his daughter, Janna, "who raised my consciousness." Did he fear feminist reproaches for his portrait of a man in troubled equipoise between a wife he honored but no longer desired and a woman he desired but would not marry?

"That's their problem, not mine," he said. "I can't begin to anticipate what they will talk about. All I hope is they talk about the book as literature."

Mr. Malamud was taken aback by one final question: Does literature do any good? He started out by saying: "It elevates, enriches, changes and, in some cases, reveals the meaning of life. In some cases, it makes you want to change your life." He broke off for a moment and then said: "I've been a teacher for 40 years and a writer for 30 years, so it's obvious to me that literature is valuable. I'd rather not answer that question. In a sense, I feel literature has proved itself; it doesn't need me to prove its value. All I have to do is say 'Shakespeare.'"

But he kept on: "It's very hard to wrestle with that question. I'll answer it something like this: Anything as important as this in life cannot fail to make some lives better than they might have been. Besides, it's fun."

Novelist Malamud: Living Is Guessing What Reality Is

U.S. News and World Report/1979

Writers are seriously concerned about the growth of conglomerates in the publishing industry. We feel that in the long run they can't help but have a censorious effect on writing. When the buck leads, the word suffers. I'm published by a small house that wants to be untrammeled, free. Nobody there attempts to censor me; nobody tells me what to write; nobody has asked me to go out and be a salesman for my books. That's how I like it.

As a result of mass interest in culture, there has been an averaging out—diminishing the very highest level and bringing up the lowest.

Some people have been elevated by their exposure to the arts; they have been influenced in good ways. On the whole, I'd rather see more people interested in culture, and I don't criticize those who can only go just so far in their appreciation. I'm glad to have them stopping to see, listen, read—thinking, perhaps, there's more to life than they had supposed.

The impulse to value the written word will endure so long as there are books to challenge readers to understand and use language with the richness and beauty shown by good writers.

Students I meet and talk with seem to want to know more than they do about literature and using the written word. Many are not satisfied with what they learned in high school. I think they would consider it a gift if they could use language more effectively and could understand its uses better. I've heard colleagues say that kids nowadays have gotten to be more serious about self-expression and language generally. I think some of them feel a sense of loss in not being able to use language with facility and eloquence.

Creativity is a complex thing. Freud considered it so mysterious that he felt unable to explain it. Maybe sometime in the future they actually will find the genetic tissue that makes it what it is. I don't want to be around when that happens. I want artistic creativity to remain forever a mystery.

Mostly, the act of writing is pure work: You set yourself to do a certain scene; you do it. If it turns out well, you feel all kinds of pleasure. If it turns out badly, there's disappointment—sometimes misery. While you're writing, there is only rarely the feeling that people who don't write imagine the writer is always involved with— namely, a kind of inspirational flow and flame.

The lives a writer invents are obviously lives that he lives in imagination: That is, he is living them as he writes. You develop your characters, and they develop themselves. At a certain point they begin to run, take off, and then you're surprised at the qualities and speed they pick up. That's part of the enjoyment of writing. Your people grow out of your conceptions of them.

I want my writing ultimately to be moving. If you move someone, there's the possibility he may change. I don't have the kind of hubris associated with attempting to reform the world, but I am out to say some things about what life is and what I think it means. In the end, I probably want to affect people in some important way relative to seeing and knowing life.

Human beings are mysterious, complex, difficult to know. Selves are locked—ultimately solipsistic, private. You're not going to know the whole truth about any one single person, ever. There's always the residue of the unknown, both in other people's lives and yours.

Human beings can't see everything. We don't know everything. We explain many things wrong. There is much that eludes us, much that's mysterious about this life and this universe. And, therefore, what we are often doing when we are living our lives is guessing what reality is. The more I experience life, the more I become aware of illusion as primary experience.

Vermont: An Inspiration for Malamud

Valerie Restivo/1980

From the Rutland, Vermont *Daily Herald*, 5 May 1980. Reprinted by permission.

NORTH BENNINGTON—Vermont honored author Bernard Malamud Saturday night, when Gov. Richard Snelling presented him with the 1979 Governor's Award for Excellence in the Arts.

It was an evening characterized by simplicity and warmth. A standing ovation followed the author's expression of gratitude.

"I like my privacy," Malamud said of his reclusiveness ". . . I also enjoy a neighbor's nod indicating he knows what I've been up to." The remark was reminiscent of the description of his latest novel, *Dubin's Lives,* of the relationship between the protagonist (a biographer) and his neighbor. The two cross paths (literally) on their habitual walks, nod and sometimes speak.

He spoke eloquently of the inspiration that has come from his 19 years in Vermont. He praised the recent enactment of anti-uranium mining legislation. He said, "The beauty of nature gets into my eyes and mind and affects my work. The contemplation of nature frees or feeds the human spirit."

He mentioned other Vermont artists he admires, among them Ben Bellitt, Louise Glueck, Robert Peck, George Clay and Nicholas Delbanco. "Not all self-defined artists will flourish here, but some will . . . I sometimes think of them as the new farmers planting seeds of the imagination, and harvesting works of art." He spoke of part-time farming and odd jobs that often mean survival. He gave a friendly plug for the state arts council, which sponsored the award ceremony and which helps some artists to survive. Unlike most other arts councils, the Vermont council is not wholly state-run; only one-seventh of its budget comes from the state.

He praised the artist's role in society: "Art seeks order. It values the human self. It tends towards morality. Artists help deepen the quality of our culture."

In presenting the award, Snelling told the writer "I celebrate your genius" and then read his favorite passage from *Dubin's Lives*. "I, too, am well past fifty," the governor confessed, expressing empathy with Dubin's post-mid-life crisis.

"'Everybody's life is mine unlived,'" he read, quoting the biographer who extends his morality by recreating the lives of others. He noted the beauty of Malamud's description of Vermont seasons.

"If Bernard Malamud has touched us with his writing—and he has—clearly, Vermont has had its effect on him."

Robert Giroux, of Farrar, Straus and Giroux, has been Malamud's editor and publisher since he began writing. Like the other speakers, Giroux waxed sentimental about the state, closing his remarks by "drinking a toast to the State of Vermont." He said "this is the first time a governor has been present" to honor a writer but that "I remember being in Dallas when T.S. Eliot was made honorary sheriff. He loved that badge." He began reading Malamud's short stories in the 1940s, in the *Partisan Review* and *Commentary*.

He recalled Malamud's first National Book Award (for *The Magic Barrel*) and complained that "the whole National Book Award has been given up—taken over by something called TABA."

He lamented the fact that "writers are no longer judged by their peers but by the publishing industry. The obscenity is that publishing is not an industry, it's a profession."

He cited the "categories" set by the new award-givers. The first is "class one" fiction and non-fiction. The second ("class two") has three categories of awards, "Novels, westerns and the third is poetry. It doesn't make as much money as 'Princess Daisy.' For the industry to put poetry after westerns is a terrible thing," Giroux said.

Malamud and Giroux held a press conference on the green and white porch of Park-McCullough House, the majestic Victorian mansion in which the festivities were held. Giroux encouraged the writer to avoid saying too much about his forthcoming novel, tentatively titled *God's Grace* and based on a character who survives a nuclear war.

"It's a fable," explained Malamud. "I have done fables before." He mentioned a talking-horse story and other short pieces and said he felt it was "time to do something more elaborate in that kind of genre." He won't say more because it's a bad policy to talk about a work in progress. "Suppose I dropped it?"

Giroux says it has happened; Malamud disagrees . . . "It wasn't dropped . . . not abandoned . . ."

"It wasn't published," the editor replied.

The writer talked of the elusiveness of details at an early stage of writing; he doesn't want to lose the strength of the project.

" . . . And you don't know what you're talking about," said the editor (referring to attempts to explain a work early on).

"It has been almost a lifetime of collaboration," Giroux continued. "He is not a writer whose hand has to be held. I've published everything he's written."

"I went to him when he was at Harcourt," added Malamud. "He couldn't get rid of me." Harcourt published *The Natural*. (Later they both changed publishers.) "It was the era of the Brooklyn Dodgers and he had it all," Giroux said with a grin. (*The Natural* is about baseball.) It operates on many levels, "there is a mythology behind it." The author used "the myth of the Percival legend." (The reader was unaware of the legend when, expecting something like *The Assistant*, she encountered the unfamiliar world of baseball.) Malamud seemed pleased to have surprised his readers. Surprise is valued highly in his world, and he prides himself on being difficult to "type."

Malamud was born in Brooklyn, N.Y., the setting for many of his early stories. He spent 12 years in Corvallis, Oregon, teaching at Oregon State University and writing *A New Life*, which is "theoretically set there," and three other novels.

In 1961, he came to Vermont to accept a position at Bennington College. Teaching is "very important" to him. "It's a way of making a living without having in any way to use my writing to make a living. There is no pressure to use my writing. . . ." He especially values the freedom to choose his subject matter apart from the reality of earning income.

He taught high school in New York City during his early years as a writer, working in evening schools, where he "was enormously taken by the diversity of the students." In Oregon, the teaching load increased and he found himself "with two full-time jobs."

In teaching writing, he sees his role as "helping people who are talented to use their talent." At Bennington College he teaches both literature and writing. He divides the contemporary American short story into two "streams of writing," the "Chekhovian and the Borghesian."

He finds that "many students haven't read enough." While he sees today's students as intelligent and talented as ever, he says they are "not as well read" as they used to be. His approach to teaching short story writing is to "teach the concept of form in the short story and ask people in the class to write their own short stories. Then there are seminars in which the other writers function as critics."

Asked what he remembers best in his own education, he recalls his years at City College (of New York) where "Teddy Goodman was a good teacher of fiction." Malamud sees education as fundamental. He has little patience with those who find it unnecessary or super- fluous. "Don't kid yourself." He values "education for spiritual growth" and finds writers who reject it "substitute their ambition for education" and are the poorer for their choice.

Giroux, too, regrets the anti-education era. "I get it in manuscripts; they can't spell."

Malamud acknowledges "the controversy over whether a writer should be in a college. Faulkner stoked a furnace for a while. Hem- ingway was a journalist . . ." (Those who call journalism another form of fiction might consider Hemingway's career all of a piece.)

Malamud Still Seeks Balance and Solitude
Michiko Kakutani/1980

The study belongs to a man who, like Yacob Bok of *The Fixer,* "liked things in place and functioning." It is an efficient room, designed for work: the books—books *he* has written—are arranged by title and language of translation on the shelves; the Danish Modern desk is covered with polite clutter. Bernard Malamud is hard at work on his latest project—a fable of sorts reminiscent of "The Jewbird" and "Talking Horse"—and this room is where he spends his mornings writing, carefully placing words on paper as he looks out over West End Avenue.

Frail, angular and resolutely austere, Mr. Malamud speaks with careful formality, emending his own statements for fluency and effect. No doubt this is an acquired trait, a palpable result of a lifetime devoted to literature: he has spent over 40 of his 66 years teaching narrative fiction; some 30 of those years writing the seven novels and three volumes of short stories that constitute his oeuvre.

"Balancing is pretty much the game," says Mr. Malamud, echoing the words of William Dubin, the protagonist of his last novel, *Dubin's Lives.* He is referring to his effort to balance his two vocations, but he could just as well be referring to his two lives: the one here in New York, where he grew up, a poor boy in Brooklyn; the other in Bennington, Vt., where he spends half the year teaching at Bennington College.

"The beauty of the city and the country is having two worlds," he adds. "And for the writer, two worlds are better than one." Mr. Malamud's achievement in letters was recently recognized by both those worlds: the Vermont Council on the Arts conferred on him the Governor's Award for Excellence in the Arts for "his contribution to literature in the state," and his alma mater, City College, gave him an honorary degree at its commencement exercises.

Whether in New York or Vermont, Mr. Malamud has led a willfully

private life. He believes that "if one goes to cocktail parties every
night, he won't find solitude," and that today "there is too much
interest in the teller, not the tale." In *The Ghost Writer*, his friend
Philip Roth created a character named Lonoff, a novelist, "deeply
skeptical of the public world," whose notions of work and esthetic
purity oblige him to live a hermetic life of solitude, and there has
been speculation that Lonoff was, in fact, a portrait of Mr. Malamud.

The theme of artistic isolation, after all, is not an alien one in Mr.
Malamud's own work; in *A New Life* the character S. Levin takes a
teaching job in the Pacific Northwest in order to escape the
emotional distractions of the city; Fidelman, the hero of several tales,
is, by the author's own description, an "artist *manque*, the man who
wants to find himself in art;" and Dubin also talks of "unity achieved
only in the work, his rainbow."

"There is a lonely element to writing," Mr. Malamud says. "You
work only with associations and words, and sometimes it becomes
enormously difficult to make the right associations and find the right
words, and the feeling you feel can be just as strong as the worries of
life, of love and family." Still, he insists that art is but part of his life
and disputes the notion that he and Lonoff are one. "It wasn't only
I," he says. "It was also Philip Rahv and, to a smaller degree Isaac
Bashevis Singer. It's fun and games for Roth—if he wants it he can
have it."

As for his own work, Mr. Malamud dismisses any autobiographical
impulse, although he is forthright in discussing the influences and
themes that have preoccupied him. From the fabulist tales of his first
collection of short stories, *The Magic Barrel*, to the realism of *Dubin's
Lives*, which emulates a 19th-century novel in its complexity, Mr.
Malamud has continually tried to challenge himself by employing
new forms. And yet there exists, in all his work, a certain idiom of
thought. It is a sense of precarious survival, of limited redemption
and, most insistently, of sadness.

"People say I write so much about misery, but you write about
what you write best," he says. "As you are grooved, so you are
grieved. One is conditioned early in family life to an interpretation of
the world. And the grieving is that no matter how much happiness or
success you collect, you cannot obliterate your early experience—
diminished perhaps, it stays with you."

The eldest of two boys born to Russian immigrants, Mr. Malamud grew up in Brooklyn. His mother died when he was 14. His father ran a small grocery, worked 16 hours a day and harbored few expectations of something better. There were no books in the Malamud home, no music, no pictures on the wall, no cultural nourishment at all, except that on Sundays the young Malamud would listen to someone else's piano through the living room window. During the Depression, he worked in the census office and a yarn factory to help support the family.

"The good thing about the Depression was everything went down to bedrock," he recalls. "Experience that deprives you of something can make you realize what it is that you need most, and it sends you inward, and that to a writer is important."

It was the advent of World War II and the Holocaust, he says, that first made him sure that he had something to say as a writer. Until then he had not given much thought as to what it meant to be Jewish, but the horror of the war—as well as the fact that he had married a gentile woman, Ann de Chiara—made him question his own identity as a Jew and compelled him to start reading about Jewish history and tradition. He realized he wanted to write. As he once explained: "The suffering of the Jews is a distinct thing for me. I for one believe that not enough has been made of the tragedy of the destruction of six million Jews. Somebody has to cry—even if it's a writer, 20 years later."

The immigrant experience of his parents provided Mr. Malamud with the world of his early stories; his father was a model for the grocer in *The Assistant*. On the basis of that novel and *The Fixer,* many critics began to regard Mr. Malamud, along with Saul Bellow and Mr. Roth, as a "Jewish writer." It is a label Mr. Malamud finds inadequate. He argues that the three writers share more differences than similarities, and he notes that in his case, Jewishness is more of a spiritual than a cultural or religious quality. "I was concerned with what Jews stood for, with their getting down to the bare bones of things," he says. "I was concerned with their ethicality—how Jews felt they had to live in order to go on living."

During most of his career, Mr. Malamud has eschewed active involvement in social issues, arguing that for an author, writing itself is involvement enough. Yet after turning 65, he says, he began to feel he should "use whatever renown I may have for some reason other than personal gratification." He compares his sense of responsibility to that of Roman senators, "who used their life experience to judge, to govern to help society." For the last year, Mr. Malamud has been president of P.E.N., protesting the repression of writers in the Soviet Union and South Africa, the rise of conglomerates in publishing and the curtailing of First Amendment rights.

Still, it is writing that remains the primary and necessary thing for Mr. Malamud. "At 66, you can't help but think about getting closer to the end," he says slowly. "I feel I've done enough now not to lose out if I don't write another book, but it's still a question of how much work can I get done in the time I have left."

Creators on Creating: Bernard Malamud
Katha Pollit/1981

From *Saturday Review,* February, 1981, 32-39. Reprinted by permission of Omni Publications International Ltd.

Born in Brooklyn 66 years ago, the son of a poor grocer, Bernard Malamud today is the celebrated author of seven novels and three collections of short stories, the holder of two National Book Awards and a Pulitzer Prize, the president of PEN, and one of the most original voices in contemporary fiction. He has written of heroism in baseball (*The Natural*) and anti-Semitism in czarist Russia (*The Fixer*), of poor Jewish immigrants trapped in failing mom-and-pop stores (*The Assistant*) and the tragi-comic flounderings of the artist manque (*Pictures of Fidelman*). His most recent novel, Dubin's Lives, the story of a middle-aged biographer torn between his wife and his young mistress, is his longest and some think, most ambitious effort.

Malamud and his wife, Ann, spend much of the year in a large white house on a quiet road in Bennington, Vermont, where for more than 20 years he has taught literature and creative writing at Bennington College. We talked in his study, a sunny, spare, functional room clearly meant for work.

Q: When did you start wanting to write?

A: Pretty early. I was always turning homework assignments into little stories. We'd be told to write a composition on Roger Williams or some aspect of life in the American Colonies and I'd make mine an adventure story. A little later, when I started going to the movies, I used to like to give long, minutely detailed, probably boring descriptions of the plots. I soon became aware I was a storyteller. I've always been one.

Q: What writers were your first heroes?

A: In my childhood, none other than the dime novelists who wrote Frank Merriwell, Nick Carter, Buffalo Bill—storytellers. I used to wait outside the stationery store for the new books to come in every other week. The joy of reading them! I really didn't get into serious reading until I was almost in college.

Q: By then you were already thinking of yourself as a writer?

A: Yes. I conceived of myself as wanting to write, without knowing what was going to come of it. This was during the Depression, and I knew I would need some kind of job right out of college. So I took courses in teaching, "education"—I hate that damn word! I also thought of studying law, but nothing ever came of it.

Q: Was there a moment in your early career—a prize, a publication, a kind word—that made you think you had a future as a writer?

A: Well, one helpful thing was winning the *Scholastic Magazine* essay contest in my senior year in high school—Erasmus Hall. I got a medal for a piece called "Life From Behind the Counter"—obviously I was already into the store, into the world of *The Assistant*. I'd been working on and off in my father's grocery since I was a kid.

Q: Was there anything in the craft of fiction, during those early years, that struck you as particularly difficult?

A: In the beginning, I didn't have much sense of the total effect of fiction, of all the extraordinary things it is capable of, and so my early stories tended to be decently plotted things that relied a lot on dialogue. Not that one comes to an enlarged vision first shot—the important thing, as someone writes, is to see that there might be in a story more than he has achieved so far, to tell himself what, and go after it. There's a gradual movement toward broader effects in my work—*Dubin's Lives,* for example, contains things I'd never done before in a novel.

Q: Where did the baseball material in *The Natural* come from?

A: Baseball was the sport I became aware of first. In my neighborhood, every night in summer, there was a crowd waiting at the corner candy store for the late newspapers with the late baseball scores. This was before many people had radios. I didn't play much baseball as a kid but I went to Ebbets Field and Yankee Stadium, I saw Babe Ruth, Dazzy Vance, and enjoyed the Brooklyn Dodgers in action.

Q: Many reviewers of *The Natural* seemed to be unable to deal with a book that worked on two levels. That must have been depressing for you.

A: It was, but you learn to read reviews selectively. You set aside those that simply don't comprehend what you're driving at. If there's just no understanding, what are you going to do? You turn to the people who can understand the quality of the book in terms of form, intention, invention. And time balances it out—today *The Natural* is taught in many American lit. courses, and of course I'm delighted.

Q: So many writers these days teach writing. Is that bad for them?

A: I don't think so. I'd advise a young writer to make a living any way he can, rather than depend entirely on writing. That way, he can be absolutely free in his choice of subject matter, and he doesn't have to worry if he writes a book that doesn't sell. I mean, he's got to keep going, to get on to his next book. So if teaching allows him to earn a certain amount of money and maintain his freedom, by all means let him teach, if he can.

Q: What about the effects of creative-writing courses on students?

A: When I go to England people say to me, "Ah, you Americans! Do you think you can teach writing?" The answer is no, you can't teach writing, but you can teach talented people; you can hasten their way through certain travails by pointing out roads that have already been taken. You can help young writers, who often have no idea what they're doing, to understand the insufficiencies of their work, and, possibly, the direction they have to go—in some cases, they ought to get out of writing entirely. What I don't approve, though, is placing too much emphasis on creative writing for undergraduates, who need an education and who really haven't found themselves yet. One creative-writing course for an under-graduate should be enough to discover whether he or she should go on or not. I'm a believer in doing it the hard way—getting into your small room, sitting at the table, excluding many of the pleasures of the world, and very seriously writing and writing, doing the burden of work that has to be done.

Q: Is this necessary isolation why so many of your characters have a sense of unlived life?

A: Isolation is an important drama for any writer, and it's bound to affect his characters. So much has to be given to the writing of a book—you *have* to shut yourself out of the variety of life. You have to make your choice, which is to stay at your desk with the book and not to regret that the day is beautiful and other people are going to the beach.

Q: And that sort of life is not for everyone?

A: Many people who go into writing do so not because they have a talent but because they have an anguish. They think their sad burdens will fall away overnight if they become successful writers. To these people, without talent I recommend no continuation.

Q: Have you ever been blocked in writing?

A: No. But I like to write about it. There's an enormous drama in not being able to find your way into a career, in confronting the mystery that prevents you from doing fulfilling work. Fidelman, for example, doesn't find what we used to call an identity, until the last sentence of *Pictures of Fidelman,* when he drops painting for glassblowing. A lawyer I know has gone into leathercraft, a stock-broker into pottery. Everyone has a desire to use some deep creative quality in the self, but sometimes they don't have the courage; sometimes they don't have enough talent to carry them through. It's almost as though the mystery shoves its hand in their faces, and only by dint of a large, difficult action are they able to get a basic insight into it.

Q: How does the germ of a fiction come to you?

A: There's no one way. Germs are independent, they come as they please.

Q: Do you go straight from one project to another, like Trollope, or do you rest between books?

A: I take some time off. Generally, between novels, I go to short stories. It's a good time to breathe.

Q: Does your daily routine change when you're at work on a book?

A: Not much; I work harder.

Q: Do you write books from start to finish, or in sections and snippets?

A: Start to finish, finish to start. I am a born reviser.

Q: Do you show your work to others while it's in progress?

A: I read to a friend, or friends. Sometimes I submit a chapter-in-progress to a magazine to see what it looks like in print, or I may read it at a public reading to hear what it sounds like in other people's ears.

Q: Do you know who your audience is? Do you write for a specific reader?

A: I write for myself and for the books and authors I most respect. I write for literature, because it moves me, and I want to be a part of it.

Q: Do people often wrongly assume your fiction is autobiographical?

A: Oh, yes. After *A New Life* I used to get letters asking whether I taught at such-and-such a place—there was a couple on the faculty who were exactly like the Gilleys. Well, they must have been visiting from the book! Where is Pauline Gilley, who is she? Don't ask me. Even informed critics make this error. After *Dubin's Lives* came out, an English critic wrote me saying, my, how difficult it must have been for you personally to write this book. Well, if the book was hard to write there were many reasons for it, but confession wasn't one of them. You won't find my autobiography in *Dubin's Lives*, although I dipped my finger—not my hand—more deeply into the autobiographical cream.

Q: You've said that *Dubin's Lives* was your attempt at bigness.

A: At breadth, at a fuller use of what I have to offer. For instance, I'd never used my love of nature so fully in a book before. Here I was able to make it part of the interior drama, and part of the mystery, too. I wanted to do more with character, also, to make life more complex, in the daily living of it, than I had done previously. And I wanted to get in more poetry, more of what is *in* me. With some fiction I read, the author doesn't really show what else he's got; he gets into a kind of Samuel Beckett mode and sings one tune forever.

Q: It's been said that a writer's first 20 years are his imaginative capital. Is that true for you?

A: There are two periods of imaginative capital, the first 20 years and the rest of your life. The first 20 years give you the world of your childhood—in my case centering around my father and mother's life in their store. The richness of *The Assistant* indicates my immersion in that world. The richness of *Dubin's Lives* comes partly from asking myself what else I knew. I realized I had never really talked about marriage, so I thought I'd better do that. Right now, I'm working on a short novel, a fable, in which God is present.

Q: You're quite prolific.

A: Well, I'm not Joyce Carol Oates.

Q: Do you know what happens to your characters after a book is finished? Do Kitty and Dubin get their son out of the Soviet Union?

A: I don't know. Their daughter marries a Sephardic Jew and joins her father in writing a book. You learn that from the list of Dubin's biographies at the end of the book. That's the thing about fiction— you set so many things in motion, because you're dealing with words, and words have a rippling effect. Each person brings to a novel the pattern of his own life, and so he reads it in a slightly different way. For example, *The Assistant* is sometimes interpreted as a mythic drama initiated by the seasons, and *The Natural* as a myth of Ceres.

Q: Does that seem far-fetched to you?

A: No, although it would be fakery to say that I had those structures in mind as I wrote. What I do say is, look what else readers have found. It's like walking in a dark cellar and grabbing something that turns out to be a bouquet of flowers.

Q: How does the future of fiction look to you?

A: Good in the long run. Fiction is often in trouble, but people respond to imagination, talent, genius for language. They're born knowing what life is about and ultimately this is what fiction tells you. You learn from the imaginative what the real world is.

A Talk with Bernard Malamud

Ji-moon Koh/1982

From Ji-moon Koh. *Major Themes in the Contemporary American Novel* (Seoul, Korea, 1984), pp. 287-296. Reprinted by permission of Ji-moon Koh.

I was fortunate to meet Mr. Malamud and have this interview after he read my article, "Bernard Malamud's Renewal of the Human Spirit," which deals with three of his seven novels, *The Assistant* and *A New Life* and *Dubin's Lives*. All of these novels are written with his own definition of art, on the basic theme of self-transcendence, exploring the idea of suffering, and with deft use of irony. The article, which will be published in the annual journal of the American Studies Association of Korea, examines the fact that the heroes in his novels have the belief that their life can renew itself and yearn for a better life, even though they get extremely caught up in isolation and suffer deep frustration. I sent the article to Mr. Malamud who was a 1981–1982 fellow of the Center for Advanced Studies in the Behavioral Sciences, Palo Alto, California. On February 2, 1982, I interviewed him at his office which overlooks Stanford University. He had many enlightening comments about art, suffering, self-transcendence, morality, democracy, freedom, love, Zen Buddhism, the image of a bird in his novels, the technique of foreshadowing, and translations. He is the author of seven novels and three collections of short stories: *The Natural*(1952), *The Assistant* (1957), *A New Life*(1961), *The Fixer*(1966), *Pictures of Fidelman: An Exhibition*(1969), *The Tenants*(1971), *Dubin's Lives*(1979), *The Magic Barrel*(1958), *Idiots First*(1963), and *Rembrandt's Hat*(1973).

In an interview with Daniel Stern, you made the following definition of art: "It [art] tends toward morality. It values life. Even when it doesn't it tends to. My former colleague, Stanley Edgar Hyman, used to say that even the act of creating a form is a moral act. That leaves out something, but I understand and like what he was driving at. It's

102

close to Frost's definition of a poem as 'a momentary stay against confusion.' Morality begins with an awareness of the sanctity of one's life, hence the lives of others—even Hitler's to begin with—the sheer privilege of being, in this miraculous cosmos, and trying to figure out why. Art, in essence, celebrates life and gives us our measure." Do you still believe in the definition?

I can say with ease that I do; that I feel that the key is in being permitted to live, being permitted to experience, being permitted to learn and to know. And I feel that this is the essence of the sheer enjoyment of life. And I feel that art teaches the same values. Art teaches that life is significant and can be learned from.

How and when did you conceive the definition? Has your view of art changed at different times?

I don't remember when I conceived the definition. I would say at a certain point it was there, and it came as a result of thinking about art, and thinking about what I was doing and trying to understand what I was doing. My view of art has changed only in the sense that it has grown. It has been pretty much the same except that it has developed in its ideas, developed in its meaning.

Please explain more in detail the reason why you strongly emphasize the necessity and importance of art in life. Does art change the world? If there were no art, would our political or economic lives be different?

Well, that's a very difficult question that you're asking and a good question too. The importance of art in life. It seems to me that there are some people who simply have no concept of the value of their lives. And one of the great and beautiful things about art is that it does teach you what the value of life and living is; what the value of another human being is; what the value of art itself is; what the value of the imagination is. I don't know that art changes the world in any way that can be very quickly discerned, but it seems to me that very slowly and in unseen ways, it changes the world only in so far as it changes the human being and ultimately art has to have that power. Those who are blind to art, of course, are not changed by it, but those who become aware of art must be changed in some way. I imagine if there were no art, that not only our political or economic, but also our psychological, philosophical and any other kind of life we had, indeed, would be different. It would be diminished.

I personally feel that suffering is the only way to solve many difficult problems with which we are confronted. I consider you a pioneer writer in exploring the significance of suffering as a mode of existence. Why have you taken a deep interest in suffering? Does this interest reflect your cultural or religious background? Have American writers been interested in this idea?

Again, a difficult question. I don't personally feel that suffering is the only way to solve many difficult problems. I would hate to have a mode of suffering imposed on people as an education. Obviously, one has to have a talent for suffering. It's nothing that comes to you without some awareness. I'm not talking about just being the victim of brute accident; I'm talking about getting something out of your experience. In *The Assistant*, I use it almost unconsciously as something that someone has to learn from. In other words, if you go through an experience, the worst thing that can happen to you is not to understand it, not to react to it, not to feel for it. If the experience is as intense as suffering, then it's wasted on the human being if he doesn't get something out of it that causes him to reflect upon his values and to reflect upon the significance of his life. And I imagine there are various reactions to suffering. As I said, there are some people who may suffer and suffer again the same way when they suffer the second or third time; and there are some people who simply become aware of lacks and losses in themselves and the fact that they could have done their living a little bit better had they tried or had been aware. And to them, once suffering educates them, obviously, they have gained something that they didn't have before. I'm not for suffering. I wish there weren't as much as there is in the world. I don't look at it as a mode of education. But I do feel that if the nature of life is to produce as much suffering as it does, then it should be the nature of the human being to learn from his experiences and to make something better of his life.

It is said that the central theme of your novels is self-transcendence. I personally think it is very difficult to define self- transcendence clearly. However, may I conclude that the way of achieving self-transcendence which is represented in your novels consists in winning

*freedom in and from the self? Why is that desirable or necessary? Are
selfishness and self-interest the same? Is selflessness always good?*

Well, I would say that, indeed, it is difficult to define self-transcendence clearly if that's what I'm saying. I'm not so sure that I like the expression self-transcendence. I like what might be called a sense of growth, a sense of, if you will, escape from the lowest levels of selfishness into a kind of generosity of spirit that makes one aware of the needs and the interests of other human beings, and perhaps even incites one to be of help to other human beings. Now, I realize that that is not easily come by and it may even sound a little bit over-idealistic, but obviously there are people who are able to keep their own interests in decent proportion and who do not intrude with selfishness, or intrude so much, I should say, with their own self-interest. Now, it's true that in my novels what I'm talking about is the whole ideal of winning freedom for the self. It seems to me that the question of why this is desirable or necessary is obvious, that the less trammeled self you have, the stronger self you have, the more effective it will tend to be. Now, I'm a little surprised by this question: is selflessness always good? I don't quite know what you mean by that. What do you mean by that: is selflessness always good?

*What I mean by selflessness is always good, first of all, is when we
think of others as the basis of our existence.*

If it's thinking of others, it's obviously good. One dislikes being preachy about these things and once you begin to assert, what should I say, the thematic value of a book, you tend to be lecturing, tend to be preaching about a mode of behavior which is in a sense derived from the fiction. I like to think of it as part of the art and not something that has been extrapolated from the art, if you know what I mean. So I'm not entirely comfortable talking this particular way, but I have no objections to what you get out of the books.

*You have defined morality as "a way of giving value to other lives
through assuring human rights," and have said that the "basis of
morality is recognizing one another's needs and co-operating." Are
morals only about how we treat others in life? Should this be our
main concern?*

Well, I have more or less answered this question in relation to the first. You remember I said when I was being interviewed by Stern that morality begins with an awareness of the sanctity of one's life, hence the lives of others, and I still stand by that. I don't think you can have morals without other human beings. So there must be something about your relationship to others. I don't know whether it should be the main concern in life. I suppose the main concern is to stay alive, but obviously one of the very strong concerns of life is to help other people stay alive.

In A New Life *you contended that democracy "owes its existence to the liberal arts." Please explain this contention in more detail.*

The liberal arts is the humanities, dealing with what is humane and what is human, and so far as democracy is concerned, of course, you deal with what is humane and human in terms of society, and that kind of society that best expresses the humane and human ideal is, to my mind, the democratic society as it best represents itself. Democratic societies can fail in their own way too. But I'm talking about democracy at its best [which,] indeed, is very much concerned with the humane and human.

You have also asserted that "the purpose of freedom is to create it for others," and that freedom "favors love." I wish to know more about your sense of the meaning and function of freedom. How do these ideas relate to Yakov Bok? Has he learned about freedom and responsibility? Is he moral?

I see freedom, obviously, as something that is within the self, or has to be achieved within the self and that freedom which has to be achieved in social terms within the society. When I speak of freedom favoring love, I feel that the condition of love favors the self, obviously, and it also favors relationships, and this is what I mean by that. It seems to me that the meaning and function of freedom in the terms in which I've just described it is more or less obvious. Now Yakov Bok has a lot to learn and begins to learn it in the present experience when he reflects a good deal on the world he lives in, his suffering, his past life, and in that way, comes to terms ultimately with the kind of self that he has been prior to the time that he is imprisoned. He is not consciously moral, but like many men, including Morris Bober, he tends to live morally because he has been in a sense educated morally. Not all people are and not all people have to be preached to to be educated morally. This is a way of seeing life with generosity and the feeling of love for others, and a sense that one is not the only person alive and that there are needs for others, obviously, that must be fulfilled. I think he is one person who, through his suffering, it seems to me, becomes a larger person.

In "The Magic Barrel" you said about love, "Love should be a byproduct of living and worship rather than its own end." And in The Assistant *you mentioned that loving "should come with love." Please explain your concept of love more concretely.*

I noticed that what you're doing in this particular quotation, that love should be a byproduct, is more or less pulling a sentence out of context from one of the short stories. I think, yes, it is "The Magic Barrel" and that doesn't necessarily represent my point of view. I simply have to say that at the beginning, otherwise anything that one of my characters says becomes a point of view of mine. It isn't. I'm merely expressing, I think it's Leo in the story who says it, to the marriage broker, and then goes on to say more. Now, loving should come with love, this too is something in the fiction itself and it's nothing that I want to preach about or comment on in any particular way.

It seems to me that you have a deep interest in Zen Buddhism. J.D. Salinger is also much interested in it. Why? Because it is similar to Judaism? Are you interested in spiritual feelings or ideas, or in some specific ideas about God and theology?

Basically, I don't have the deepest interest in Zen Buddhism. I needed it in *Dubin's Lives;* I read up on it; and I learned about it, and was able, I think, to use it. On the other hand, I am interested in ideas about God and theology and however these ideas are expressed interests me, and therefore I am interested to that extent in Zen Buddhism.

I personally feel that the concepts of morality and freedom examined in your novels tend to express almost the same idea: that other people should be recognized and respected. This similarity of concepts is also to be found in other contemporary American novelists. Why is this consensus established? Is the idea of mutual respect compatible with capitalism? Does the idea get lost in a multi-ethnic, multi-racial society?

I imagine that the similarities in concepts occur because many of us read the same things and have been educated in the democratic way. I think people like Bellow and, in his way, Mailer, and Updike, even though they have a difference in political thinking, still are very much alive to an understanding of the important values, as one would say, these things we are talking about—morality and freedom and all that sort of thing. It becomes established because it is there for you to find, and if you find it, it is valuable to you. As for mutual respect compatible with capitalism, whoever thinks of it in terms of capitalism? This is a mode of being and one is; he doesn't try to figure out whether capitalism has anything to do with it or interferes with mutual respect in any way. I mean one tolerates capitalism, and capitalism is no great idea of democracy or any aware mode of living. I suppose the idea does manage at times to get lost when you say a multi-racial society, you don't say a racial society. Various people come to ideas with more fullness and some people come to ideas with less fullness; and some come, obviously, with more comprehension and others with less. I don't think it's the ethnic and racial element that does it; it's the quality of the human being to respond to certain important aspects of human life.

You published your first novel, The Natural, *in 1952, and your most recent novel,* Dubin's Lives, *in 1979. For these twenty-seven years many major events in your society have taken place. For example, the Cold War, McCarthyism, the assassination of President Kennedy and Martin Luther King, the Vietnam War, President Nixon's resignation, and the ERA movement. How have you been influenced by these events in your writing? Which interests you most, which least? Are you very political? Do you consider yourself liberal or conservative, socially? politically?*

It's very hard to use the elements of the history of a society, no matter how important they are in any given novel; yet, almost all of these events have been touched in either stories or novels. For example, the Cold War, or something like it, is referred to in a short story called "Man in the Drawer." McCarthyism rears its ugly head in *A New Life.* I haven't dealt with the assassination of Kennedy or Martin Luther King. But I have dealt in a sense with the Vietnam War, [in] two short stories, "Man in the Drawer," and "My Son The

Murderer," and not with Nixon's resignation but the personality of
Nixon in *Dubin's Lives*. I haven't touched the ERA movement yet,
but there is hope.

*You use frequently the image of a bird in your novels? Why? Are
there other favored images or symbols or motifs? Do these change in
type or in meaning over the years?*

Well, birds to me I suppose are symbols of freedom. So far as
favored images are concerned, that I leave to you to find in my work.
I'm sure that there are others. I'm sure that symbols change as well as
grow, in the sense that they do grow and there must be, what shall I
say, the collection of symbols throughout the years as one becomes
aware of phenomena which he then turns into metaphoric use.

*It seems to me that you make a deft use of the technique of
foreshadowing. Why do you like this technique so much? Is this just a
traditional technique of narrative or a special way or perspective of
viewing life?*

I think I do like foreshadowing; it's a way of creating drama before
the fact, and I remember, I think I became aware of foreshadowing
for the first time when I was a student studying the plays of
Shakespeare. The concept of foreshadowing, as I said, seems to
excite me as a mode of creating a drama before a drama. And I'm
afraid I have since then been foreshadowing.

*Has the function or the form of humor changed in your work? Do
you see life as essentially comic or tragic? Or both, or neither?*

I think humor exists in my work and that is the main thing.
Obviously, humor is part of life; humor has to be there. I would be
very, very unhappy if I could not see the comic elements that exist in
life and in fiction. So let's say that I'm on the watch, on the look for
comedy and I will haul it in by both ears whenever I can.

*Which do you think is the best one of your novels? Why did you
write more short fiction at one time? Did you find larger, more
complex subjects required writing novels instead?*

I think I write what I feel like writing. And if I feel like writing short
stories, then I write them; and if I feel like writing novels, I write
them. I don't have a best novel, even though I'm aware of the fact
that there are people who seem to like one over the other. I can't join

that little enterprise. I hope to be able to write some more short stories in the near future now that I've finished my latest novel. Okay?

Are you writing another novel? Do you see your writing moving in new directions? Are your interests changing?

I have just completed another novel which I call *God's Grace*. I think when you read this you will see that my interests have moved, let's say, in an unanticipated direction. I hope my interests are changing; I hope they've become more varied and more interesting as I go along. Obviously, from these interests one takes the source of whatever book or story he happens to be working on.

Do you have any good advice for foreign students who are going to read your novels?

My only advice is that they read the novels carefully and if they don't understand them the first time, please to read them a second time. And also, I hope they enjoy them.

Some of your novels have been translated into other languages. Do you know anything about the adequacy or aesthetic success of these translations, and do you think it is possible for a work of fiction to be translated with reasonable fidelity to the original meanings of the writer?

I've looked into some of the novels, some of the translations of languages I can more or less read. And sometimes I've been very happily pleased and sometimes I've been dismayed by translations that are not reasonably faithful to the original meanings of the book. I'm absolutely certain that there are gifted translators who can do a good deal of justice to any given book in any given language. The main part or the main thing is to have the good luck to get such a translator.

God, Bernard Malamud, and the Rebirth of Man

Curt Suplee/1982

From *The Washington Post*, 27 August 1982, F1, F8. Reprinted
by permission of *The Washington Post*.

OLD BENNINGTON, VT. How to explain it—the agony and obligation of
the thing? "Well," says Bernard Malamud, "let me tell you a joke."

A good and pious old man falls on hard times. He goes to the
synagogue, beseeching God to let him win the lottery in exchange for
his years of faith. He leaves optimistic, but after nothing happens, he
returns and pleads again. Still God remains silent, the supplicant
poor. Finally he goes back a third time, infuriated now, railing at
Jehovah, "Why don't you give me a break?" Suddenly the voice of
God arises in a wind, and says to the man, "Why don't you give *Me*
a break? Why don't you at least buy a ticket!"

Malamud isn't laughing. After all, man's abdication of virtue and
inhumanity to God are the subjects of his new novel—the most
unusual and certainly the riskiest he has written. But at 68, after 11
books including *The Magic Barrel, The Fixer* and *Dubin's Lives,* after
the Pulitzer Prize and two National Book Awards, he has outfaced
fear. "And that's why in *God's Grace* you see a man who is not afraid
to write about God's role in the universe."

The apocalyptic gloom of his subject seems hopelessly out of place
in this cheery, sun-washed house, a rambling white-frame idyll near
Bennington College, where Malamud has taught for 20 years. A
comforting percussion of cooking sounds comes from the big kitchen
where his wife Ann, a chipper dynamo of a woman, is devising lunch;
on the porch an old tiger tomcat lolls ingratiatingly; and in the
distance the cloud-dappled foothills of the Green Mountains hover
like a Yankee daydream.

And Malamud himself—still frail from a recent illness—at first
appears an improbable Isaiah. With his tidy demeanor, incessant self-
editing ("no, wait, there's a better word . . .") and deadpan, scrup-
ulous style, he could be the most successful CPA in Westport. He is

111

uneasy with talking about himself ("that kind of stuff, it's not up his alley," says his friend Philip Roth) and seems reluctant to start. He pauses to choose among several pairs of glasses, then sits down carefully, feet flat on the floor, long fingers knitted in his lap. Finally, with the anxious geniality of a brave man settling in for root canals, he says, "Now then, I think we can begin."

God's Grace combines a Miltonic ambition of theme with the vernacular crackle of comic dialogue. It begins with the destruction of mankind by nuclear horror and global flood, leaving one accidental survivor, a Jewish scientist named Calvin Cohn, adrift on a ship in the ocean. God appears to acknowledge the error ("though mine, it was not a serious one; a serious mistake might have jammed the universe") but condemns Cohn, too, to eventual death because man has "defiled himself": "They have destroyed my handiwork," God intones, "they tore apart my ozone, carbonized my oxygen, acidified my refreshing rain. Now they affront my cosmos. How much shall the Lord endure?"

Thus indicted, Cohn and a shipboard chimp named Buz drift onto an Edenic island where they discover a variety of other monkeys and Cohn attempts to rebuild civilization by educating them, issuing seven Admonitions in lieu of commandments. The story is freighted with biblical parallels and allusions to accounts of human evolution by anthropologists such as Louis Leakey. Topics familiar from Malamud's earlier fiction—racial hatred, moral despair and the hope of trans-ethnic understanding—here find simian counterparts. (Buz becomes a crucifix-toting intellectual whose moral neutrality borders on sadism.) In the end, bestiality proves intractable and the fledgling society convulses in predatory lust and blood sacrifice.

The idea for the book arose when a colleague at Bennington arranged for a private printing of Malamud's two previous animal fables, "The Jewbird" and "Talking Horse." "I thought, why not go at a novel with animals as the major characters." Ever since Aesop, he says, it is "the ultimate imaginative act to create a creature—no wait, there's a better word—a living being who is not human and yet can talk, giving you the opportunity of presenting a miracle in every sentence he speaks."

And the theme had been in his mind for years, "the sense that I had that man was in trouble," that "man in many ways was a disappointment to himself." Not simply the nuclear nightmare, although "the fears that have arisen through 20th-century technology are horrendous. They've scared many of us out of our shoes. We're running even when we're not running." Not only the fact that "we haven't conquered some of our major evils—racial hatred, bigotry, intolerance." But also what he calls "the deceitful devaluation of man" in our age, the failure of culture to respect the individual soul— and of that soul to value itself—that is "one of the great sins of ourselves and our society." So man is "despised of God—he loses his favored status in God's eye and thus loses the world."

He researched the book by reading Jane Goodall on chimps, and evolutionary treatises from Darwin to Stephen Jay Gould, and concludes that Cohn's efforts are "within the realm of possibility—so much is being done, new experiments on animals, on language in animals, in a sense I'm just taking the next step." And if the book's gore-sodden denouement seems bleakly pessimistic, Malamud leaves a note of hope in George, a gorilla named slyly after one of the human precursors whose skeleton was discovered by Leakey. "The reader, if he's looking for a positive view, has to look around that."

Novelist John Hawkes, who has known Malamud for 20 years, says that "for a great, well-known writer to risk this kind of book seems absolutely marvelous." Risky indeed. There is an obvious peril in unleashing a deeply earnest and uncomplicated animal fable on a critical establishment steeped in cynical post-modern realism. Already John Leonard in *The New York Times* has said it "groans under the weight of its many meanings . . . I find myself tired of masks on clowns." Nor are the unflattering treatment of Christianity and emphasis on evolution likely to delight Moral Majoritarians.

"I'm prepared to accept all kinds of disappointing criticisms," says Malamud. "I've heard the book described as gutsy, and that's okay with me. In fact, I think all my work is subsumed under that rubric." He still relishes the outraged mail following *The Assistant,* with its unsentimental look at shop-weary immigrants and its Italian charac- ter, Frank Alpine, who first robs a Jewish grocer, then works for him, then converts to Judaism. "One of the earliest letters I got was from a Jewish gentleman who wrote, 'Your father must be whirling in his grave!'"

His parents were Yiddish-speaking Russian immigrants who had a

small grocery store in Brooklyn. Malamud says he was the bene-
ficiary "not of having happy parents, but of having *good* parents,"
who instilled in him the necessity of "doing well by others." He might
never have become interested in language but for a bout of
pneumonia that nearly killed him. When he recovered, his father in a
fit of joy bought him a 20-volume *Book of Knowledge*. In grammar
school Malamud wrote stories, mesmerized by exotic words like
"Sargasso Sea," regaling his friends with lavish recountings of movies
"to save them a dime." Unlike the squalid and perilous urban
tableaux of his fiction, Malamud recalls the neighborhood as
"unexciting." It did not contribute to his widely esteemed ear for
ethnic dialogue—"That's a gift, that's where I was lucky. We had a lot
of musicians and actors in the family"—and left him only with "a
hunger to be in the country" (which he satisfies six months of the
year at Bennington before wintering in a rented apartment in New
York's West 60s).

He had decided to be a writer well before enrolling at City College
of New York in 1932, but spent his twenties in a series of factory and
retail jobs and worked as a clerk in the Census Bureau here. In 1940
he entered Columbia University's graduate school, and after teaching
high school at night for nine years, took a teaching job at Oregon
State, still without a published book. "In many ways, I am a real child
of the Depression. There was no money around, and until I could
support my family, I didn't know what to do with my art. That's the
force of my strength of obligation. I am in many ways a strong-willed
man."

His son, Paul, 34, an editor at the United States Information
Agency in Washington, agrees. His father forbade television in the
house until the late '50s to encourage Paul and his sister Janna to
read. And he set an example of "incredible and absolutely consistent
discipline," reading every night in his slow, methodical way,
underlining frequently. While shaving he would suddenly think of a
sentence and "then he'd call out of the bathroom and ask me to
write it down in his notebook," Paul Malamud recalls. But he "always
kept a clear separation between his work and his family, and always
insisted that the whole family sit down and have dinner together."

He similarly insists now that work will stop for lunch, served with
relentless bonhomie by Ann, who in shuttling back and forth

frequently calls out questions, blithely interrupting her husband in mid-sentence. Malamud defers obligingly, even seems glad of the pauses. "We haven't had many visitors here lately," he says, meticulously peeling his peach. It's not simply that he's recuperating under Ann's solicitous ministrations. Even after the Pulitzer Prize, "he tried not to be a celebrity," says Paul Malamud. "He doesn't prize material things all that highly, and the center of his life has always been his family and friends."

He's "the kindest person imaginable, terribly, terribly generous," says Hawkes. The two men meet often to read their work-in-progress to each other, and once when they were out walking in Bennington, they encountered a "terribly confused" young person trying to find the address listed in a help-wanted ad. "Bern listened patiently, and then began going from house to house. He spent about half an hour until he found the person who put the ad in the paper."

Malamud's work is infused with baleful but robust humor, and Paul Malamud says his father "has a Swiftian streak in him" which leads to the "kind of acerbic, satirical quality" apparent in *God's Grace*. But "one of the surprising things about him," says Hawkes, "is that he's generally quite, quite serious, a man of spirit." Indeed, Malamud's mind veers inexorably to the abstract. Ask him for a specific exemplification, and he pauses, blinks toward his lap, and returns an answer equally general, often religious.

In Malamud's cosmology, free will and an omnipotent deity coexist because God ("who invented man to perfect Himself") has an overall plan "to make man meet his obligations, but in a way he can't tell him about in advance—to make him use himself best." Not surprisingly, the same paradigm recurs when Malamud talks about literature. (The first story, says Cohn, was "God inventing Himself.") After devising the thematic scheme and social topicality, he lets his characters range free in his imagination. "That's how an inventive writer earns his living. I can't outguess my characters all the time, although God knows I try. But when I get a character to surprise me, then I know I'm cooking with gas.

Malamud's genius is to capture the soul-scorching flashpoint at which painful self-discovery becomes moral epiphany. "Self-under-standing is a very strong theme in my books—working to penetrate the mystery of the self." Often his protagonists are impoverished Jews

whose clashes with gentile hostility force self-awareness and spiritual
re-birth, leading many critics to regard Malamud chiefly as a "Jewish
writer." But "that's a reduction of my accomplishment. It diminishes
something." ("*All* men are Jews," he once said, and "Jews are the
very *stuff* of drama.") Still, he is invariably compared to Nobel
laureate Isaac Bashevis Singer. "Don't lump me in with Singer. We're
very different." And although he often writes of largely ineffectual
victims, "I don't go in for the schlemiel interpretation of my work.
There's a difference of intent. I have not given up the hero—I simply
use heroic qualities in small men. Sometimes my characters do things
so heroic that I myself blanch at their accomplishment." He cites the
example of Frank Alpine in *The Assistant*. "There ought to be more
heroes than there are. Idealism has become a strange word."

His subjects are as protean as his themes are universal. In his
baseball novel, *The Natural* (1952), he limned the soulless rapacity of
an all-American Iago in a thicket of symbolism, then turned to the
world of poor Jewish shopkeepers for realism in *The Assistant* (1957)
and spare spiritual parables in his first story collection, *The Magic
Barrel* (1958). "When *The Assistant* and *The Magic Barrel* first
appeared," says Philip Roth, "I was a young university instructor, and
the originality of that imagination was a revelation to me and my
friends. Malamud, like Bellow, was somebody we'd been waiting
for."

The Magic Barrel earned Malamud the National Book Award, as
did the Dostoyevskian pathos of *The Fixer* (1967), based on the
infamous Russian Beiliss case of 1913. His evocation of dogged
dignity in the face of brutal anti-semitism won the Pulitzer Prize for
fiction. "*The Assistant* should have gotten a prize too," Malamud
says. "But it was the same year that Cheever wrote *The Wapshot
Chronicle* and I don't think anybody even *looked* at *The Assistant*."
Still, the awards considerably "strengthened my sense of my own
worth and helped me to get into material I wouldn't have touched
until then." For example, the vicious cultural clash between blacks
and Jews in *The Tenants* (1971). "I expected trouble, but I didn't get
it," although some black writers complained that Malamud had no
business portraying a violent black character's search for identity.
Malamud, too, had initial qualms. "But I've overcome enough of

them to make me a free man. I think of my fiction as a free man's fiction.

He changed subjects radically again in 1979 with *Dubin's Lives,* about the mid-life crisis and sexual longings of a bookish biographer whose obsession with D.H. Lawrence helps him rationalize an affair with a Benningtonesque barefoot hippie named Fanny at the expense of his long marriage. The texture and structure were a reversion to 19th-century forms, reflecting his admiration of George Eliot and Thomas Hardy; the themes self-exploratory ("What had my experience totaled up to? What did I know up to this point?") although not autobiographical. As he wrote in his journal for the novel, "One must transcend the autobiographical detail by inventing it after it is remembered."

However, despite his love of Russian and English 19th century fiction, "my whole history as a writer is in connection much more with American literature than any other kind." In fact, in his realistic treatment of the morally fabulous, he much resembles Hawthorne. Malamud is suddenly animated. "That's what Lionel Trilling said!" and he is abruptly up and padding toward a bookcase. "Let me just get it here." He pulls down the volume, returns to his chair, and begins to read, finger tracking the paragraphs: "dreamlike massiveness . . . theocratic cultures . . . life to be lived in control of the sterner virtues."

Ann Malamud appears, leaning through the doorway to tell her husband her schedule for the afternoon. He nods, stops, and with the self-conscious formality of a man for whom no emotion comes cheap, says, "I realize how dependent I've become upon you, and I'm grateful for all you're doing. I'm not ashamed to say it."

"Oh well," she says, eyes down. "It's nothing. All in a day's work."

For a long, soft moment they look at each other, and then she gently closes the door. They have been married 37 years.

Malamud says it still "haunts me that I'm not a better writer, that I could have taken better advantage of some of the opportunities I gave myself." One of them is his next project. "I have never gotten over an old desire to write a play," and he's rewriting one that appeared in the story collection *Idiots First* (1963). He is not teaching this year, but Bennington allows him to do as he pleases, and

Malamud values the refuge. "I've never lived around a lot of other writers. Although I want that kind of stimulation, I don't want to make that kind of sacrifice to get it. I use the school to protect me and my vision of the world. But in the best of all possible worlds, I wouldn't recommend it. I'd advise a writer to live his life as fully as he can, and then write about it.

He writes by hand, then revises on an ancient black manual typewriter, and admonishes his students to attempt "the most daring elements of fictive life." That usually precludes six-figure sales. But "the division of the spoil takes on an importance greater than it should. Writers don't know what their true business is," and an author has to "get used to the idea of never becoming a wealthy man in a country where wealth means a lot."

Farrar, Straus and Giroux is only printing 30,000 copies of the novel, down 20,000 from the press run for *Dubin's Lives*. Malamud is resigned. "It's a very sad, difficult time for writers," he says, and an author can easily become dispirited from "the sale of his books, competition from television and the demands made on him to produce the kind of books that will sell in droves." Publishers, he says, often require depressingly little: "I want more than that. I want the publisher to come to the writer with joy and respect and a sense of the miracles he's engaged in." No matter what the reviews may say. "There was a time," he says, "when I was too much concerned with what people were saying about my writing" and "I learned that I must throw reviewers off my back."

"But now," he says, and suddenly 30 years of discipline and hard-won pride are swelling his voice, lighting his eyes, "I've come to a point in my life—sacrificed my youth coming to it—where I know my work is strong."

Malamud's Sense of Despair

Leah Garchik/1982

From the *San Francisco Chronicle Review,* 5 September 1982, 1, 9. Copyright © San Francisco Chronicle. Reprinted by permission.

In the beginning, on page one, God talks to Calvin Cohn. He's made a sloppy mistake, He says; He hadn't intended that Cohn would survive. Working at the floor of the ocean during a thermonuclear war, remaining undersea during the flood that followed, Cohn has escaped the final holocaust: he is the last man on earth.

Thus, Bernard Malamud starts his eighth novel, as a grieving Cohn shakes his fist at the sky, God made us who we are, he rages. How can man be responsible for the devastation?

It's a philosophical and ethical question that has plagued Malamud for 37 years. In a conversation early this summer, when the author was just finishing up a year at Stanford's Center for Advanced Study in the Behavioral Sciences, he said that the question of "what this meant for the future" had been on his mind "since the first atomic blast . . ." The fact that mankind so readily skipped to the brink of suicide, where it has teetered menacingly ever since, "proclaims a certain insufficiency of man's that I can't make peace with." Whether this impending doom was brought upon [himself] by man or ordained by God is the central subject of *God's Grace.* But the God Malamud sees, although all-powerful, is more a symbol of fate than a theological figure. "It has nothing to do with religion," he insists. When Calvin Cohn rejected his father's legacy in the rabbinate, he turned from religion to science; he is a paleologist. But cast ashore—with Buz, a chimpanzee trained aboard the research vessel—on a small island, Cohn cherishes the relics of his heritage: his father's recordings of traditional Jewish songs, stories from "Tales of the Hasidim," his skullcap. He reads aloud to Buz from the Bible.

Malamud and God have dealt mankind a crushing blow, but they have also provided a miracle. Cohn discovers that Buz had been taught to speak. After he spliced a pair of copper wires embedded in the chimp's neck, he has a companion with whom he can converse.

119

The feat is improbable, but it works as a fictional device. "Once (the talking animal) is established, the reader will believe anything," Malamud explains. After the reader believes that a beast can converse—as readers of his previous stories, "The Jew Bird" and "Talking Horse" did—the author is freed from the constrictions of reality.

Readers will be surprised, too, by Malamud's treatment of Calvin Cohn, a major break from his past characterizations. Fans are familiar with the author's stories about writers, about day-to-day angst, romance, life under politically oppressive regimes. They were stories about *men* and their life-long fears. Often the specter of Malamud's own personality was discerned lurking in the shadows of his protagonists.

But Malamud maintains that Calvin Cohn is a character quite apart from previous renditions. "Calvin keeps his distance. I let him keep his distance . . . I let him be himself." This is a story about *mankind*; the fears Malamud expresses go beyond the length of an individual life. They are fears for the fate of humans in all eternity.

As the story unfolds, Cohn's character is revealed by his actions. We come to know the man by his deeds, for instance, when Malamud has him prepare a Passover seder in the wilderness.

This is one of the most moving and funny sections of the book. The seder participants are Cohn, Buz, five new chimps that have turned up on the island and George, a resident gorilla. "Cohn had more or less forgiven him for destroying his father's record—'Kol Nidre,'—nothing less, a sad loss—probably George had thought the record was a licorice wafer or something equally good to eat," he writes.

During the course of the ritual, Buz, who has been trained by a Christian scientist, crosses himself. Cohn chastises him, pointing out that the gesture is inappropriate at a seder. When they toast to their prosperity in the coming year, later in the ritual, Buz wishes for freedom of religion.

The genre of this story, which combines supernatural fantasy, and philosophy, is very different from his past fiction. But "fiction tends often to tell you what fiction can do. You think that it's unbelievable, except that you believe it."

Malamud is concerned that critics may dwell on the medium more than the message. "I expect anything will happen. (They'll say) 'Malamud has done something new, something he hasn't done before.' That 'Malamud has extended his own animal stories.' That I've taken chances with this particular fiction that are greater than any chances I've taken."

All true, but those chances were considered risks. "I am a daring writer." Malamud felt that the subject matter was so grave that the issue had to be raised directly. This story is less a metaphor than an absolute depiction of the author's worst fears. "I felt I had to deal with God in a more direct way, because of the subject matter. I was giving God a greater opportunity to participate in the action."

He's also aware that the subject is weighty, that he may be accused of sermonizing. But "the theme (of nuclear war and annihilation) is so outspoken" to him that he eventually overcame an author's natural inclination to symbolism, to openly include "the thematic material that I felt was implicit in this particular story. I was really concerned with not doing it too brazenly."

This subtlety applies not to the setting of the book—Malamud's own sense of despair at the present state of the world is evident from the start—but to its denouement. "I'm pessimistic about the future . . ." he said. "I'd gotten to the point where I had to say something openly and strongly, more so than I ever had before. Political activity is one thing; a work of art is another. I have in no way sacrificed the art at the expense of the message."

Malamud has carefully pondered the difficulties of the genre, the characters and the subject. "As a writer, I tend to know what I must do to achieve. One never always knows; one mostly knows." It's a stunning story, all the more powerful because of this reserve. At the close of the story the reader is left still pondering the basic question: is mankind responsible for this terrible fate or is God? Malamud has broached the subject and he's not embarrassed to explore it, but he lets the reader find his own answer.

He succeeded in doing exactly what he intended to do: not exactly to chastise the human race, but to sound a warning, to prod, to force the reader to come to his own conclusion.

For Malamud it was a matter of "fighting it out with yourself about what you could represent and what you could bring that is new. That struggle is ongoing and only you can solve it. I'm 68 years old and

I've been writing since I was a kid. In all those years I have learned something . . . The secret to becoming a good writer lies in the self, in self-study, discipline, maturity; in constantly seeking the highest opportunities to do well."

Last spring, Malamud took an afternoon away from editing his galleys, he said, to talk to a class of writing students at Stanford. He told them what he thought good writing demanded: " 'Dig down and dig in.' And some of them believed it."

In *God's Grace* he has followed his own advice, digging down to "do something as a writer that I've carried within me."

And he has dug in, attempting to write "more deeply, more interestingly, more fully" than ever before. When we talked, on that sunny afternoon in June, Malamud chose his words precisely, honing his remarks to say exactly what he wanted to say. Without bravado, he remarked, "I try not to let the art of writing down." In *God's Grace* he hasn't.

Malamud's Long View of Short Stories

Karen Heller/1983

From USA Today, 19 August 1983, 30. Copyright © 1983 USA Today. Reprinted by permission.

OLD BENNINGTON, VT.—On a day of dappled sunlight, the summer sun streaming through lush, verdant maples, Bernard Malamud opens the door of his white gingerbread house and invites a stranger in.

The writer, who is thin, freckled and slightly tanned, displays a quiet graciousness, a sense that he is pleased to have this interruption in his daily routine. His wife, Ann, a woman of seemingly limitless vivacity, joins him for a lunch of ham and egg salad sandwiches, lemon sherbet and blueberries, on a porch that overlooks the majestic Green Mountains.

Afterward, there is a long talk about books (his and others'), and a leisurely walk around this southern Vermont town.

All of this comes as a surprise. Not Malamud's generous nature: that is evident in his writing, repeatedly chronicled by colleagues. No, it is a surprise because of Malamud's penchant for privacy, which is legend.

Talk does not come easily at first—he fidgets for almost an hour—but as the afternoon ages, the 69-year-old writer speaks like an old friend.

Malamud has won two National Book Awards (for *The Magic Barrel* in '59 and for *The Fixer* in '67) and the Pulitzer Prize (again for *The Fixer*). In May he received the American Academy and Institute of Arts and Letters Gold Medal for fiction. His first short story, *The Cost of Living,* was published in *Harper's Bazaar* 34 years ago. His most recent, *The Model,* appears in this month's *Atlantic.* In October, Farrar, Straus & Giroux will publish these, among others, in *The Stories of Bernard Malamud.*

"These are my best stories," Malamud says with a quiet pride that is recurrent throughout his conversation and always appropriate, never jarring. "The collection includes 25 stories. There are another

15 (that he's written). Throughout the years I've noticed how often these stories are selected to be reprinted." Of the book, Malamud says: "It was about time."

Malamud does not worry for the future of the short story. "I don't find it's in trouble in any sense of the word," he says in his soft-shoe voice. "They say that about the novel, too, and then the next genius comes along and destroys it."

Malamud's most recent novel, *God's Grace*, was published last fall. It is a daring book, an instructive fable about the sole human survivor of a nuclear holocaust and a family of talking simians. "The novel begins with a gorilla talking. *That's* different," he says. "If you don't take those risks, you won't learn."

Now, Malamud is working exclusively on short stories. "The novel takes a lot out of you. You live longer with a novel. . . . That's one of the pleasures of the short story," he says, speaking slowly, searching for the right word. "The payoff is faster. The effect may be startlingly right."

Many of Malamud's short stories, and some of his novels as well, are about immigrant Jews who are more European than American, more Old World than New. They have the timeless quality of old tales and myths.

"I am a universal writer. I think I'm generally recognized as that," he says. "People abroad recognize my writing."

The subjects of his novels range from baseball to a Russian prison to a New England college [sic] to the last man on earth. "But there is some sense of me in all of them, even in *God's Grace*. It's my given experience. I'm merely addressing a vital but not necessarily limited experience." Of the differences from one book to the next, Malamud surmises, "I am an inventive writer."

He always wanted to write a play ("I've done a scene of it"), and he once toyed with writing a biography. Of D.H. Lawrence, just like the hero of *Dubin's Lives*? "Oh, no, there are too many of him," he says. "A biography of Mahler."

Malamud lives the summers and falls in Vermont; the winters in his apartment on the West Side of New York. Next month he is off to the Bellagio Study and Conference Center in Italy, the Rockefeller-endowed retreat for scholars.

"You have to be invited," Ann Malamud says with obvious pride.

She can hardly wait. "Ann's family is Italian," Malamud says. During lunch she drops a few Italian phrases into the conversation, rolling her r's like a *senora*.

He was born the son of Russian immigrants; his father was the owner of a grocery store in Brooklyn. Malamud decided to be a writer while still a child, though his first novel wasn't published until he was 38. After graduating from the City College of New York, he held retail and factory jobs, clerked at the U.S. Census Bureau, taught high school at night. He was a professor at Oregon State for 12 years before moving to Vermont to teach at Bennington College in 1961.

He liked teaching—he now teaches an occasional class—but one senses he did it to enhance his writing. "You have to know what you know, what you've got, and how to use it best," he says. "I tried to write as well as I could. That's what I did best. . . . Many young writers give themselves a greater leeway this side of discipline. Many young writers claim they are interested in writing with freedom. It isn't freedom. It's something closer to self-indulgence."

Still, he has a need to experiment. "There's so much in your work to cover. If you stay locked in one place you don't grow," he says. "I like to work from city to city, from garden to garden, writing about what I know. One thing I always ask myself when I shut a book, I finish it, is, 'What else do I know?'" He is smiling, squinting in the summer sun.

The Natural, Bernard Malamud's first novel (1952), is being filmed in Buffalo, with Robert Redford starring. It isn't the first time one of his works has been translated to the screen: Alan Bates starred in *The Fixer* (1968); Zero Mostel in *The Angel Levine* (1970).

The Natural "was the experience of being a kid in Brooklyn," says Malamud. "I lived somewhere near Ebbets Field. The old Brooklyn Dodgers were our heroes, our stars, like out of myths. Since the stadium was that near, it had to concern you. You were concerned with the accomplishments of various mythological heroes."

Though removed from the project, Malamud is happy to see it being filmed. "*The Natural* has become a legend. It amuses me that now it is coming to the screen in another guise," he says. "That suits me. That pleases me."

Malamud is also pleased Redford is playing hero Roy Hobbs, a natural innocent and baseball talent who comes up from the minors to make baseball history—and scandal.

Says the author: "I believe Redford will be very good when Roy Hobbs gets that second wind, when he's standing there at the plate and that look, that inspiration, comes across his face. Yes, he'll be good at that."

What delights Malamud most is that with the movie's release, the book will be readily available in bookstores. "The only thing I want is an active reading," he says. "The true fact is the book. That's the gorgeous fact—as Henry James might say."

An Interview with Bernard Malamud

Joel Salzberg/1983

This previously unpublished interview took place in New York City on 21 June 1983 and is published with the permission of Joel Salzberg.

Q: Someone in 1979 who had just finished reading *Dubin's Lives* might have some difficulty in predicting the turn your fiction was going to take in *God's Grace.* When did the subject of your last novel come to you?

A: *God's Grace* had been on my mind before I wrote *Dubin's Lives.* At that time, however, I had not yet figured out how I would use chimpanzees as characters, nor had I worked out the structure of the novel.

Q: Did *God's Grace* possibly have its source in anything you had written before—for example, "The Jewbird" or "Talking Horse?"

A: I'm sure it had. As a child I had enjoyed fantasies about talking animals and later read some medieval beast epics. Along with my previously written animal stories, it eventually led to *God's Grace.*

One of the misreadings of the novel, by the way, is that it ends in tragedy. Some reviewers have failed to recognize that a gorilla recites *Kaddish* for Calvin Cohn, and that is indeed a cause for optimism; the prayer itself is a vehicle of God's grace.

Q: Are you still as optimistic about the future of man as you were earlier in your career?

A: I have moved from optimism about man to a new and serious understanding of how growth and achievement take place. Growth is slow and man must fight for it.

Q: Women do not seem to have the same prominence in your fiction as men. They may have important roles, but they are never at the dramatic center of your work. Have you ever thought about doing your own version of *Portrait of a Lady*?

A: Imaginations differ. Because of James's own unique upbringing, and his special relationship to his mother, the subject of *Portrait of a Lady* probably came naturally to him, however, this is not the kind of

127

novel that I am inclined to write. Yet the death of my mother, while she was still young, had an influence on my writing, and there is in my fiction a hunger for women that comes out in conscious ways.

Q: You seem to have a special interest in some of your characters—Arthur Fidelman, for example. Is there anything beyond coincidence in the fact that Fidelman's name is also that of your mother's brother? Was your uncle in any way a source for your character?

A: Fidelman was purely an invention and was not consciously modelled on any living character. He appealed to me because he allowed me to explore the subject of vocation. I was attracted to him as a version of the failed artist.

Q: Do you ever find yourself thinking about Fidelman, or any of your characters, and discovering new things about them?

A: Fidelman is complete as he is, and it is best for a writer to look forward. The function of the writer is to involve himself in some kind of continual pursuit for the meaning of individual lives and from them to come up with new subjects.

Q: I recently read that *The Natural* is going to be made into a film. Will you be able to influence the direction this production takes? I understand that you were not happy with the making of *The Fixer.*

A: The movie rights to *The Natural* were originally sold to someone who in turn sold them to Robert Redford. I will have no say in the production of this film. As for the movie of *The Fixer,* I did not care for Dalton Trumbo's treatment of the novel, and the use of color interferes with the conception of reality I wanted to convey in the novel. The starkness of pre-revolutionary Russia would have been more appropriately rendered in black and white. To my mind, *Angel Levine* was also a failed movie because of its sentimental characterizations and stereotyping. A terrible burden is placed on the short story when the narrative structure is changed for the sake of extending the time of the film.

Q: You have indicated in other interviews that you enjoy taking risks? What do you mean by that?

A: *The Fixer, The Tenants,* and *God's Grace* are examples of my taking risks. This means provoking the imagination by using my art as a stimulus. If you take a chance you may go somewhere you haven't been to before.

Q: To what extent has the Holocaust influenced your work as a writer? Have you ever felt compelled to make a direct response to the Holocaust in your fiction?

A: I am compelled to think about it as a man rather than a writer. Someone like Elie Wiesel who had a first-hand knowledge of the experience is in a better position to write about it than I. He has become a voice for those people who could not communicate their personal experiences and emotions.

Q: Would you name some of the contemporary writers who have a special appeal to you?

A: Günter Grass, Saul Bellow, V.S. Naipal, Gabriel Marquez are writers who illuminate the world they see and bring something new to the art of writing; they are gifted, serious, and daring.

Q: Have you ever found the critical writing about your work interesting or helpful to you?

A: A book has a bedrock of meaning, and I keep that in mind when I write, but I would not interfere with imaginative criticism if the critic can demonstrate to me that he has read my book carefully. I enjoy interpretation wherever it goes and critical variety up to a point, that point being idiocy.

Q: To what extent has the fiction of Henry James influenced you?

A: James's imaginative richness fitted in with my own literary fantasies. His mind was prolific and just. He demonstrates a variety of fictional possibilities and his work may provide a good education for a writer.

Q: Do you have a sense of what the teacher of literature ought to be teaching or discussing in the college classroom in 1983?

A: The function of the teacher is to encourage his students to read more fully and with greater awareness. The whole purpose of literature is to excite the mind to go beyond itself. Literature must not forget the problems of the moment, but it must create a form by which it can relate to other eras whose problems may have been different from ours. Simple ideological answers are inadequate. "Literature is a rush of richness in the direction of imaginative thought."

Bernard Malamud: Morals and Surprises
Helen Benedict/1983

From the *Antioch Review*, 41, no. 1 (Winter 1983), 28-36. Copyright © by The Antioch Review, Inc. Reprinted by permission of the Editors.

"The purpose of a writer is to keep civilization from destroying itself," Bernard Malamud once wrote, and in his new novel, *God's Grace*, his intention is exactly that. The book, a fable published last September by Farrar, Straus & Giroux, is a dire warning against the perils of nuclear war and against that force within us that drives us, literally, to destroy ourselves.

"I have been concerned with this almost since the first atom bomb was dropped on the Japanese," Malamud said in a telephone interview from his house in Vermont, where he is recuperating from a serious illness. "I remember the horrid feeling I had then that the beginning of an evil time had occurred. I have a sense now, as many people have, of peril—it's terribly frightening. I feel it is the writer's business to cry havoc, because silence can't increase understanding or evoke mercy."

Malamud has written about man's struggle against destructive forces before. In his second novel, *The Assistant,* shopkeeper Morris Bober struggles against crushing poverty; in his most famous work, *The Fixer,* Yakov Bok struggles against the forces of anti-Semitism that try to destroy his freedom and his will; and in *The Tenants*, white writer Harry Lesser struggles against habits of racism when he tries to be friends with black writer Willie Spearmint. But in *God's Grace*, Malamud's eleventh book, the destructive force is the most absolute of all—nuclear war—and Malamud's conclusion the bleakest of all—utter devastation.

God's Grace opens the day after nuclear war has destroyed civilization and all mankind, and the earth is smothered in one enormous flood. God, however, overlooked one man, Calvin Cohn, a paleontologist who was poking around at the bottom of the sea in an oceanography vessel when the bombs blew. Cohn survives to struggle against a world destroyed by war and against that invisible force of evil in the soul that has led man to destroy himself. As God explains to him, "I made man free, but his freedom, badly used, destroyed him."

"The question of man's freedom has always interested me," Malamud said. "How much of the freedom does he have? How far does it extend? And ultimately, what does he do with it? It's the last part that bothers me most. I'm not going to gainsay man's accomplishments, but I still feel that there's a vast sense of failure that has clouded his best efforts to produce a greater freedom than he was born with."

Cohn floats on the ocean for a while, bemoaning his fate, when he discovers a companion. A baby chimpanzee named Buz has survived with him. They find an island and soon several more apes appear, who all, through some unexplained miracle, learn how to talk. (Why can they talk? How have they survived? Is this some mysterious game of God's?) Cohn tries to do just what Malamud suggests writers do, what he is trying to do himself with this book—stop civilization from destroying itself. He sets up a school under a tree and every day he teaches the chimps all he knows about history, science, morals, philosophy, and religion. He especially focuses on the wickedness of mankind.

"The reason I may seem to dwell a bit heavily on the negative aspect of man," he explains uncomfortably, "is to give you something to think about so you may, in a future chimpanzee society, avoid repeating man's worst errors. The future lies in your hands."

Cohn, however, is tempting God's wrath by playing with fate like this, by trying to create a new race, by, in a sense, playing God. Also, he can't resist blaming God once in awhile for man's destruction. If God made man imperfect, he thinks, and man's imperfection led him to self-destruction, then whose fault is it? "Why didn't the Almighty do a better job?" He even argues about it with God once in a while:

"WHY DO YOU CONTEND WITH ME, MR. COHN?" God booms from the sky.

". . . I humbly ask to understand the Lord's intention."

"WHO ARE YOU TO UNDERSTAND THE LORD'S INTENTION? HOW CAN I EXPLAIN MY MYSTERY TO YOUR MIND? CAN A CRIPPLE ASCEND A FLAMING OF STARS"

"Abraham and Job contended," Cohn heard himself say.

"THEY WERE MY SERVANTS."

"Job complained You destroyed the blameless as well as the wicked."

"JOB THEREFORE REPENTED."

"Job is a myth."

"MYTH ME NO MYTHS. I AM THE LORD THY GOD."

Cohn shook his enraged fist. "You have destroyed mankind. Our children are dead. Where are justice and mercy?"

Holy Moses, he thought. What am I doing to myself. Am I deranged?

Cohn's audacity causes him to live in fear of being struck down at any moment, and the reader lives it with him throughout the novel. By the end, Cohn has indeed gone too far. The destructive forces within and without him have caught up. The chimps revert to savagery, Cohn and his teachings are destroyed, mankind is finally extinct.

"The book asks, in a sense, a simple question," Malamud said. "Why does man treat himself so badly? What is the key to sane existence?"

This is not the first time Malamud has asked such questions. As Philip Roth once wrote of him, "What it is to be human, to be humane, is his subject; connection, indebtedness, responsibility, these are his moral concerns." He has never, however, asked them this pointedly before, nor at such a politically appropriate time—in the face of the rising possibility of nuclear war.

God's Grace is not only a serious book, it is funny. "Even a reader of holocaust drama has to be enticed into the act of reading, or he may feel he would rather forgo the anguish," Malamud said. "Not all of us are eager to be reminded of how close man has come, through his own madness, to the end of time. So, I wanted a little laughter in this serious book." He has it. The humor, some of Malamud's best, makes the novel an instantly enticing read. Especially funny are the passages when Cohn talks back to God. At the beginning of the novel, for instance, when God finds out that Cohn has survived, they have this conversation:

"And that you, Mr. Cohn," thunders the irritated God, "happen to exist when no one else does, though embarrassing to Me, has nothing to do with your having studied for the rabbinate, or for that matter, having given it up."

Cohn ignores this reprimand and tries to bargain for his life. "Lord . . . it wasn't as though I had a choice. I was at the bottom of the ocean attending to my work when the Devastation struck. Since I am alive it would only be fair if You let me live. A new fact is a new condition."

If Malamud were in Cohn's position, would he talk back to God like that? "Of course I would! There's a whole tradition of back-talk from Adam to Job. God may not enjoy man as much as we would like Him to, but He seems to enjoy the human voice." (With all this talk of God, one wonders if Malamud is seriously religious. All he will say is, "I think it was Carlyle who said whether he believed in God was his business and God's." A very Cohn-like answer.

The chimps provide comedy for the novel too, but they don't work as well as Cohn and God. Indeed, when Buz first appears, it's a little disappointing—the promise of a novel about Cohn alone in an empty world, the way Yakov Bok was alone in his prison cell, some of Malamud's best writing ever, is broken. Also, the chimps are some-times just too cute, verging on the Walt Disneyish. This is especially true of the female chimp, who is so stereotypically feminine that she reminds one of the fluff-headed Dora in *David Copperfield*—all pout and lisp. (Her sex scenes with Cohn are bound to raise a few horrified eyebrows among readers, incidentally. They may even get the book banned, along with *The Fixer*, where the Moral Majority holds sway.) However, the interaction between the apes and Cohn becomes lively enough to make up for their occasional corniness. As Malamud said, "Talking animals can, in a sense, be exciting people."

The chimps, it turns out, not only represent the newly born race of savages in the novel, perhaps much as we must have originally been, but Christians, and so Malamud, true to form, brings in religious questions. The only ape who chooses to share Cohn's Judaism is a lumbering gorilla of questionable intelligence named George, who, like his predecessors, is rejected by the Christians. The symbolism of this—Christians as savages, the Jew as a lonely, kind-hearted outcast—might well offend some people, but Malamud does not believe in explaining his work, even to smooth ruffled tempers. To explain, he says, "destroys the art." "Why Buz is interested in Christianity and George in Judaism is their particular business," he said firmly. "But I like what has come out of it—the imaginative quality of their relationship to each other."

Malamud had the idea for the apes around 1975, while he was working on his last novel, *Dubin's Lives*. "I had done a couple of short stories about animals," he said. "One was called 'The Jewbird' and the other 'Talking Horse,' and I wanted to see how far I could go with that in a novel." This experimentation is typical of Malamud and is one of his earmarks as a writer. In his past books, he has jumped from black militants to Russian Jews to Italian gangsters, written about magic and realism, and has tried everything from stream-of-consciousness to almost scientific prose. Very few contemporary authors have taken such risks with their careers.

"I wanted to see what I could do," Malamud said. "I felt that the nature of talent is difficult to define and that one way of trying to define it is to see what it can do.

"You know, some people felt that *The Fixer* was written out of some compulsion I had to deal with the fate of the Jews. It was a serious novel, but in essence it was, like my other books at the time, somewhat experimental. Can you do this, can you do it well? Those were the major questions I asked myself."

Malamud's books, as wide-ranging as they are, can be roughly divided into two types, the modern-life novels and the Jewish books. The modern-life novels, which are either not about Jews or are about men whose Jewishness is incidental to them, tend to be less believable, lively, or well-written than the others. In *The Natural*, for instance, Malamud's first novel about Roy Hobbs, a baseball star who keeps making the wrong decisions, the gentile hero never quite becomes three-dimensional. *A New Life*, his third novel about an alcoholic college professor who tries, and fails, to improve his life, is so accurate about academics that it is flat and dull. And *Dubin's Lives*, about a middle-aged biographer who nearly wrecks his marriage by falling for an unprepossessing student half his age, has long sections that stretch credulity to the snapping point.

The Jewish books, on the other hand, *The Assistant, The Fixer, The Tenants, Pictures of Fidelman,* and his three volumes of short stories, are more poetic, moving, and humorous than the others.

They are also the ones that have won Malamud his awards—two
National Book Awards, one for *The Fixer* and one for a book of
stories, *The Magic Barrel,* and a Pulitzer Prize, also for *The Fixer.*
God's Grace rates with these better Jewish books, although its flaws,
particularly the clichéd chimps, prevent it from reaching the level of
his best short stories or of *The Fixer,* his most successfully executed
book of all. Malamud, however, does not like having his books
characterized as Jewish, compliment intended or not.

"Jewishness is important to me, but I don't consider myself only a
Jewish writer," he once said in an interview. "I have interests beyond
that, and I feel I am writing for all men." In the same interview he
added, "All men are Jews, except that they don't know it. I think it's
an understandable statement and a metaphoric way of indicating
how history, sooner or later, treats all men."

This is certainly true in *God's Grace.* Nuclear war is a holocaust for
us all.

Whether he likes it or not, however, Malamud has always been
considered one of America's major Jewish writers, along with Saul
Bellow and Philip Roth. ("Bellow pokes fun at this sort of thing," he
once said, "by calling Bellow-Malamud-Roth the Hart, Shaffner, and
Marx of Jewish-American literature.") He has not reached the acclaim
of Bellow, because his work has been so uneven in quality, but he is
more respectable than Roth, having produced more and avoided
stooping to Roth's vulgarity. In writing about *The Assistant* for the
New York Times, Morris Dickstein explained the Jewishness of Malamud's work. "Malamud had distilled what seemed like the emotional
essence of first-generation Eastern European Jews, stoic, self-
abnegating, mildly hysterical, passionately familial—all done with a
sureness of touch that makes Bellow and Roth seem assimilated, and
whose only peer, it seems clear today, is that anachronistic survivor,
I. B. Singer."

Malamud is not as immersed in Judaic culture and tradition as
Singer, however. He can embrace a Yiddish idiom or leave it, write of
an old world or new. When he was asked by Israel Shenker to
describe a typical Malamudian character for the *New York Times,* he
said, "A Malamudian character is someone who fears his fate, is
caught up in it, yet manages to outrun it. He's the subject and object
of laughter and pity."

This describes a character with more hope, more courage, and a little less foolishness than the recurring schlemiel in Singer's works. Yakov Bok, for instance, emerges spiritually triumphant after imprisonment and torture at the hands of anti-Semites in czarist Russia. But, just because Malamud has avoided the archetypal schlemiel does not make his writing any less Jewish. As Dickstein wrote, "Though *The Assistant* and *The Magic Barrel* boast no character like Portnoy or Herzog monomaniacal enough to become a cultural byword, they have claims to being the purest expression of the Jewish imagination in American literature."

Malamud's preoccupation with the question of how man uses his freedom, how he tries to "outrun" his fate, is expressed in many of his books through the metaphor of a prison, from its most literal in *The Fixer* to its most abstract—Cohn's solitude on earth. "It is a metaphor for the dilemma of men throughout history," Malamud once explained to critics Leslie and Joyce Field. "Necessity is the primary prison, though the bars are not visible to all. Then there are the man-made prisons of social injustice, apathy, ignorance. There are others, tight or loose, visible or invisible, according to one's predilection or vulnerability."

Malamud's first figurative prison, the grocery store in *The Assistant*, his second novel, came from his own experience. His parents, Russian immigrants who settled in Brooklyn, made their living by running such a store, and when Malamud's mother died when he was fifteen, he had to spend more time than ever confined behind the counter. Anyone who reads his early stories of grocery-store life will never again be able to enter one without feeling guilt and pity.

Malamud first began writing when he was a teenager working in that store—he used to turn his homework into stories—and many of the settings for his fiction since have been drawn from his life. The Brooklyn shopkeepers and Jewish immigrants came from his childhood; the blacks in his stories "Angel Levine" and "Black Is My Favorite Color" and in *The Tenants* from his days teaching in Harlem when he was thirty-four; the academic life in *A New Life* from his twelve years teaching in Oregon; the material for his Italian stories and *Pictures of Fidelman* from the year he spent in Italy with his wife of Italian background, Ann de Chiara; and finally, the Vermont setting for *Dubin's Lives* from his present home in Bennington, where he has been living and teaching on and off for twenty years.

Although Malamud began writing when he was young, he did not publish in major magazines until he was thirty-six and already married with a son, Paul. This was mainly because much of his twenties were taken up with getting a bachelor's degree from City College in New York and a master's from Columbia University, and with working in such places as factories and stores to support himself. "I had written a few stories in college, [and] after graduation I began to write again," he has explained. "The rise of totalitarianism, the Second World War, and the situation of the Jews in Europe helped me to come to what I wanted to say as a writer."

In 1949, when he was thirty-five, Malamud was offered a job teaching English at Oregon State College in Corvallis, so he left his home in Greenwich Village and moved there with his family. Because he had no doctorate, he was in an insecure position at the college, just as Levin is in *A New Life,* but eventually he earned the position of associate professor. It was in Oregon that his career took off. He published in several major magazines in 1950, and in 1952 his first novel was published and his daughter Janna was born. Four years later, he received a *Partisan Review* fellowship, which he used to go with his family to Italy. "Through my wife's relatives and acquaintances I was almost at once *into* Italian life and got the feel of their speech, modes of behavior, style," Malamud once wrote. "When I go abroad I like to stay in one place as long as possible until I can define its quality."

The Malamud family remained in Oregon until 1961, when Malamud was offered a position teaching in the Division of Language and Literature at Bennington College. Despite his success as an author, he has continued to teach throughout his life, either at Bennington or as a visitor at various other campuses. "I'd advise a young writer to make a living any way he can, rather than depend entirely on writing . . ." he once said. "So if teaching allows him to earn a certain amount of money and maintain his freedom, by all means let him teach, if he can." Malamud has also traveled a lot around Europe and to the Soviet Union, where he went to research *The Fixer.* His story "Man in the Drawer," from *Rembrandt's Hat,* also comes from this visit.

When *Dubin's Lives* came out in 1979, readers were quick to assume autobiography because it was set in Vermont and was about a man near Malamud's age, but Malamud says he no more than

"dipped" his "finger into the autobiographical cream." He denies
ever having been an autobiographical writer—no strings of disguised
Malamuds are to be found in his works. "In essence, a writer sooner
or later becomes almost all the characters in his novel," he said, "but
I can't measure how strongly I project myself into a character I'm
inventing. I can't insist on it because of the need for distancing
myself."

That Malamud will never reveal the autobiographical elements of
his fiction is indicative of his privateness. For years at the beginning of
his career he refused interviews and he has always kept his family life
well out of the public eye. "I know that ours is supposed to be a
confessional age and that much gets said trippingly off the tongue,"
he said, "but my feeling is that if one tells all about oneself, there's
nothing left to tell."

Is this attitude a reflection of Malamud's increasing lack of interest
in himself as he grows older? "Unfortunately, I don't find myself less
interesting at all!" he said, laughing. "I feel I'm more daring in certain
ways and braver than I've been, and even less foolish." Then he
added seriously, "I haven't lost my fears, but I'm less fearful about
life. I ask far more from it than I have in the past."

Is Malamud so much harder on Cohn than his previous heroes
because he expects more from life now? Poor Cohn only gets to
"outrun" his fate for a short time, he is denied the triumph of Yakov
Bok, and God's Grace has a bleaker conclusion than any of Malamud's other books. Is he more pessimistic about man's fate than he
was when he wrote The Fixer?

"Yes, I am more pessimistic than I used to be," Malamud said a
little sadly. "I feel that the more the world stays the same, the worse it
seems to become. Man seems to be a constant disappointment to
himself." He hesitated a moment, then added quietly, "In a sense,
blaming man gets you nowhere. But, on the other hand, whom else
can you seriously blame?"

Malamud's Last Interview? A Memoir

Joel Salzberg/1986

From *Studies in American Jewish Literature,* 7, no. 2 (Fall 1988),
233-239. Copyright © 1988 by The Kent State University Press.
Reprinted by permission.

Whether my telephone interview with Bernard Malamud on January 27, 1986, was indeed the very last that Malamud was to give before he died less than two months later, on March 18, 1986, I have no way of knowing. But the proximity of his death to the date of my forty-five minute phone conversation with him lent an air of finality to his dry, paternal, and slightly pedagogical voice that sometimes alternated between kindness and annoyance. That voice was also notable for projecting its own cadences into those of a self-effacing Jewish widower, of making death sound like a Jewish longshoreman, or of rendering God's voice as that of an aging and irritable Jewish academic.

When my wife told me that Bernard Malamud had called our home in Boulder, Colorado, ten minutes before I had returned from a Saturday morning run, I felt a sudden rush of apprehension. I had included my telephone number in my last letter to him confirming our arrangements for a telephone interview which we agreed was to take place in late February, and it was only January 25. I had no reason to expect to hear from him except in case of a conflict in his schedule or possibly for health reasons. In June of 1983, as I was about to begin my first interview with him at his apartment in New York City, he mentioned in passing his recent bypass surgery, and so the spectre of poor health was in the back of my mind as the reason for his unexpected call. In any event, he left his New York number with my wife and a message for me to contact him immediately.

I dialed Malamud's number a few minutes later and was caught off guard by Ann Malamud's amiable and unexpected *shalom.* Having exchanged only momentary pleasantries with her in her West End Avenue apartment just prior to interviewing "Bern" in 1983, I felt that replying in kind was a liberty or an unwarranted intimacy not to be taken despite her friendly greeting. When Malamud did get on the line, he said that he had to reschedule our interview for a date earlier than February. What necessity prompted the change was never revealed in our brief exchange that I can recall. The revised date for the interview turned out to be January 27, 1986, at 4:00 P.M. New York time—only two days away. Our previously agreed on format was for Malamud to look over in advance twelve to fifteen questions before the actual interview, but that arrangement was now abandoned. The remainder of my weekend would be devoted to devising questions that I hoped would elicit something new or unexpected for inclusion in the introduction to Critical Essays on Bernard Malamud, a collection that I was currently editing for G. K. Hall.

I called Malamud at the scheduled time and we exchanged greetings. When he replied to mine, I was surprised at his frank admission that he was not altogether well, but he did not elaborate. In my forty-five minute conversation with him, I became painfully aware of his struggle to remain Bernard Malamud the writer, the self that had slowly and methodically evolved from the boy who wrote short stories in back of his father's grocery store. If I were hoping for fresh insights into his life and work, they did not materialize, although during the interview I unexpectedly encountered a Bernard Malamud who, in his frustration, anger, and kindness, might have been a character from his own fiction.

There is a widely held impression that Malamud did not grant many interviews. Yet from 1958, the date of his first interview with Joseph Wershba, Malamud, in fact, gave over thirty which were published in full, a number that seems unusually large for a writer who was highly reticent, if not occasionally crusty about discussing either his personal history or interpretive questions regarding his work. He had in the past acknowledged some awkwardness and inhibition in the presence of a tape recorder, usually insisting that it not be used in the interview; one of the few instances that I am aware of in which he allowed his answers to be taped was in his 1975 interview with Daniel Stern for The Paris Review, a concession to friends who were honoring him on his sixtieth birthday. If Malamud was often ambivalent about giving interviews and generally approached them with caution and reserve, the large number that he did give—and the many questions that he responded to in letters (some of them on file at The Library of Congress)—suggest some deep personal need to reach out to audiences beyond the scope of his fiction. Nevertheless, he had just as comparable a need for privacy. Over the years he had not offered any amplification of the terse and unadorned facts about his early childhood and his relationship with his father, mother, disabled brother, and stepmother. That privacy extended with equal rigor to his adult life. There is, perhaps, an irony in his resistance to such an inquiry, at a time when his own increasing fascination with biography led him to explore the lives of D. H. Lawrence, Virginia Woolf, and Alma Mahler and to render in fiction what he called "biographical essence." Nevertheless, I began by risking an autobiographical question which he quickly dodged. But moments before my questioning began, Malamud himself took the initiative, as he had done in our previous interview in 1983.

Malamud: Let's begin by my asking you a question. What about the ground rules? . . . I don't want to do this word by word.

(The ground rules had, in fact, been established in an earlier letter. I was to submit a transcript of our conversation which he would edit in order to represent his ideas and language as accurately as possible. His question, however, seemed less a matter of forgetfulness and more a ritual of self-protection. When I had satisfied him, we began.)

Interviewer: In your most recently published story, "A Lost Grave," your character Hecht refers to himself as "a late bloomer," and I believe that expression occurs elsewhere in your work.

Malamud: Anything about me as a late bloomer, I prefer not to deal with. . . . My desire to keep my personal life out of this is the desire of any sane man who has lived over seventy years. . . . I am going on seventy-two this April.

Interviewer: I am perhaps making you more sensitive than you need to be. Let me continue, then, with other examples of your most recent work, "In Kew Gardens" and "Alma Redeemed." What were your reasons for choosing to write about Virginia Woolf and Alma Mahler? What intrigued you about these women as characters for fiction?

Malamud: "Virginia Woolf" was the course I gave at Bennington College. I read a lot for the course, and I became very much interested in Woolf as a human being, a writer, and a genius. I wanted to deepen my understanding of her, and I felt that I could do it by putting together an enormously simplified life of a very complex woman. I knew I was taking a chance, but I thought it was a chance I should take. Now with Alma. . . . There is something very personal here that I can't go into at present.

Interviewer: Technically, these narratives are quite different from your other pieces of short fiction, but do they have any connection to that work?

Malamud: I feel that their connection to my past work has something to do with my interest in almost all human beings, and Virginia Woolf and Alma Mahler as especially interesting human beings. . . . But the thought eludes me, and I don't want to pursue it haphazardly. Let me try to enlarge on that a bit later.

Interviewer: Has Virginia Woolf, either through her own life or through her characters, offered you any insights that you have applied to the creation of your own characters?

Malamud: No, I don't think so. She doesn't give me any particular insight into my characters. I have an understanding of who they are and where they came from, and there is little that she can offer me with her kind of world which is so different from my kind of world. My interest in Woolf is, in some degree, related to the problems of writing.

Interviewer: Let me pursue this question from another angle. From your earliest fiction critics have observed that many of your characters appear to be almost wedded to some private grief from which they are inseparable. Did you perhaps feel a certain empathy with Virginia Woolf because of her own absorption with such grief or of corresponding feelings in her characters?

Malamud: That might indeed be true. There is no question to me at this moment that there is truth in it, even before I have had the chance to puzzle it out. . . . But I would have to think about it.

Interviewer: In discussing *God's Grace* with me in 1983, you felt that some critics had misread the book in regarding it as entirely pessimistic. . . .

Malamud: I had to find a way for man to have a possible future.

Interviewer: Granted that you might have intended to end the book on a note of optimism, do you disagree with those who feel the book is filled with anger, and that it is an anger towards God as well as man?

Malamud: That is indeed a subtle question. All I can say is that anger is not an unlikely reaction of a writer living in the times that we do. When I talked to you in 1983, I hadn't really figured out fully Calvin Cohn's relationship to God. Obviously he has one if he can talk with him at the beginning and make his complaint and indictment. . . . You know one thing that I don't like about what we're doing is that I have begun to explain my fiction, and I don't like to do that. . . . For years I have avoided answering questions of this kind. That does not mean to say that I never answered them, but when I did it was happenstance. Someone might have asked me a question, and on a certain day I was less guarded and more relaxed. And indeed I would answer the question, and there you have a contradiction that is not really a contradiction. . . .

Interviewer: I realize that I have taken certain risks in raising some of these questions with you. . . .

Malamud: You know, Nabokov would not take questions of this kind. . . . He and his wife would first read through them in advance and decide just what part of a question did not threaten him. I used to laugh a little about that, but now that I am on the receiving end, I have a better understanding of his situation.

Interviewer: Would you be willing to comment briefly on the work you are now engaged in?

Malamud: No, it's a book in the making—you don't monkey with that.

Interviewer: Let me just ask, then, if the book represents a new direction in your work?

Malamud: No question about it. It's one of the things that has me on tenterhooks about whether I can make it come off. . . . I am reminded of a question that someone asked Matisse about the transformation that took place from his earliest to his latest work. He replied that he felt anxiety every time he was trying to paint something new and later astonishment after seeing his work successfully completed. Whenever he felt that anxiety, he had to reinvent himself into existence by taking chances he had never taken before. . . . I feel as though I'm in a similar situation. Right now I feel pressed against the wall for having to deal with these questions. I find it difficult to express myself when I am scrounging, as it were, to state the terms of a new book.

Interviewer: Why are you still giving interviews at a time when you have a much greater priority? It seems that both now and in the past you have been torn between a desire to discuss your work and a need to remain private. Have you been able to balance the two?

Malamud: Not always successfully. There is in me a certain kindness. I like to be of assistance if I can do it in a way that doesn't threaten me as an artist. Being an artist is the central fact of my life, but it is not the only fact. . . . [The formal interview ends.]

It was not an easy time for either one of us. Malamud seemed to struggle with his answers, and he was obviously unhappy with some of my questions. At one point I offered to forget the interview for the present, and after hesitating for a moment, he decided to continue. This interview, however, blessedly dwindled into casual conversation, taking an unexpected personal turn, as Malamud began to interview me. Eventually he returned to his own work in progress with some wistfulness, as we exchanged goodbyes and good wishes. My conversation with him contained no great surprises, except in my becoming an unexpected, if not unwilling, witness to his vulnerability. While his health was only mentioned at the beginning, perhaps his greatest underlying fear—and a thematic preoccupation in much of his fiction—was the loss of creative powers, a diminishing of the self as personally harrowing to him as either death or a universe without God.

With the exception of one or two allusions to the interview in the introduction to *Critical Essays on Bernard Malamud,* I had originally decided against using any part of it, but with Malamud's death, the interview took on new meaning, as perhaps his final public utterance, preserving a few last moments of his unique voice, style, and per-sonality. With the exception of several mechanical changes, I have attempted to transcribe as faithfully as possible Malamud's own idiom. His closing words, "I like to be of assistance," are uninten-tionally reminiscent of the theme central to his earliest fiction, an appropriate way for him to sign off.

Remembrances of Malamud: 1972–1986

Evelyn Avery/1990

This recollection of conversations with Malamud was written especially for this volume.

Bernard Malamud had died. At 72 one of America's finest writers and a treasured friend, had, after several years, succumbed to the effects of a heart attack and stroke. Although aware of his poor health, I was still unprepared for the news of his death. Dejected, I recalled our relationship, begun in Oregon in 1972 and continued until our last visit in Baltimore in November 1985. Unfortunately, my memories yielded only fragments which refused to coalesce, a tribute to the complexity of Malamud and his work.

An internationally famed author, he was remarkably unaffected and accessible. When I first wrote to him about my thesis on the fiction of Richard Wright and Bernard Malamud, I described the parallels between my life and his work. "Please keep writing since I want to find out what will happen to me next." Within three weeks, he replied from England. "My dear Mrs. Avery, you keep well and I'll keep writing. We will compare notes in the future."[1] Within two years, we had the opportunity to do so in Oregon where I was a graduate student and where he had taught for a decade at Oregon State University. After a reading at the University of Oregon, Malamud attended an English department dinner reception.[2] In person he seemed smaller, more vulnerable than in his book-jacket photograph. Somewhat shy and wary of crowds, Malamud had positioned himself to the side and spoke quietly but firmly to a faculty member. "I am not an ethnic writer," Malamud said, "but neither do I write abstractly. Often, I write from a particular experience, sometimes from Italian or more frequently Jewish, but always to communicate with general readers, not just with certain groups."

[1]Bernard Malamud note to Evelyn Avery, April 1970.
[2]Bernard Malamud, University of Oregon presentation, 3 August 1972.

Shaking his head, the English professor reminded him of his statement "all men are Jews." "Isn't that an example of imposing an ethnic identity on non-Jews?" he asked. Malamud replied with a sigh. "I never expected anyone to take it literally. It's a symbolic way of showing how history, sooner or later, treats us all." To the professor's request for an autograph, he good-naturedly agreed, suggesting that in the future the scholar read an author's novels, not the critics' fiction. As I moved towards him, he held out his hand. "You must be Mrs. Avery. I have been looking forward to this meeting since you wrote."

Nearby, my thesis advisor had just learned from my husband that I was pregnant. "Her thesis may never be completed," he worried aloud. To my surprise and to those around, another voice spoke up. "Life is more important than art, mazel tov," Malamud said, extending his hand to my husband and patting my shoulder. For the rest of the evening we talked about literature, his writing and our respective childhoods in Brooklyn. Asked about influences, he pointed to Russian writers such as Dostoyevsky and Chekhov, and American authors, Nathanial Hawthorne and Henry James. "What about Yiddish writers or earlier Jewish-American ones?" I asked.

"Of course I am familiar with Sholem Aleichem and fellow-writers like Saul Bellow and Isaac Singer. But I don't think they have influenced me. Mostly, my ideas come from my imagination and from random experiences, perhaps some from the passionate Russian authors."[3]

"What about the impact of your background on your writing?" I asked. "Certainly, some of my values and even details can be traced to my experiences." As the son of a poor Russian Jewish grocer, he observed his father's honesty and hard work often go unrewarded. Malamud also remembered lit candles, the holidays, Yiddish words and accented English, which influenced his writing, defining his "Yinglish" style as well as contributing character types. However, his family was not religious, in part a consequence of a gruelling work schedule, but also an emphasis on Jewish values rather than rituals. "My father," he said, "was a good man, though poor, a 'mensch,' who treated all people fairly. Perhaps he inadvertently encouraged

[3]Bernard Malamud to Evelyn Avery, dinner reception at Dr. Bartel's house, Eugene, OR, 3 August 1972.

my interest in the world beyond the ghetto. Still I want to remind you," Malamud said, "that while all authors use autobiography, for me that's only a jumping-off point."

The autobiographical issue surfaced a year later in our correspondence about *The Tenants,* which focused on two writers, one black and one Jewish, and related to my dissertation on Richard Wright and Bernard Malamud. Malamud responded generously to my questions:

The characters and events are fictional. However, different cultures have always interested me. I remember seeing black basketball players at the Flatbush Boys Club in Brooklyn. Athletic and graceful, they enjoyed their game and made me like it and admire them. I also appreciated the pretty black girls in brightly colored dresses, but I had a sense of them as people with a fate of their own. I was aware of anti-black feeling in the vaguest sort of way. Basically, I felt sympathy for them in a diffused, apolitical way. I used to make it a point to sit next to blacks on the subway. I remember a certain sadness and a strangeness. Perhaps it was just the fear of the other man's differences. Perhaps these were feelings I worked from in *The Tenants* and also provided material for "Black Is My Favorite Color," and "Angel Levine."

To my comment that the critics were not particularly perceptive about *The Tenants,* he noted that "they tend to confuse fiction and life. They looked for a political statement; but I write literature not propaganda. Some even viewed the ending as bleak, while I offer reconciliation before it is too late."[4]

Although we continued to correspond, it would be years before we would meet again. I hesitated to intrude on his tight writing schedule but needn't have worried. Malamud, I learned, led a full life which included a devoted family, good friends, rewarding students and a lively interest in the world. He was, with the help of his wife, Ann, highly capable of arranging his priorities so that writing was primary but not exclusive. Despite his reputation as a private, reserved person, he was a considerate host. When I wrote him that my family and I would be touring New England in July 1977, he responded

[4]Bernard Malamud letter to Evelyn Avery, 8 July 1973.

immediately, inviting us to visit him at his home in Bennington, Vermont, where he taught half of the year.

The evening before our appointment, we were scouting the area for his house. Since it was dusk, I had difficulty identifying the slender man on the side of the road until he spoke. "Mrs. Avery, welcome to Bennington. How was your trip? Have you found a place to stay? So these are the sons who competed with your thesis for your attention."[5] Both his questions and a concern for our comfort were voiced sincerely. Before we parted, he urged us to call his wife for further information about the area.

The next day we drove up to a handsome, sprawling white house, surrounded by an expanse of lawn and tall, lush evergreens. We were greeted promptly by the writer in casual slacks and a short-sleeve shirt. Balding, with a fringe of grey hair and a brushlike moustache to match, Malamud looked more like a businessman than the self-conscious artist or intellectual. His slightly gravelly New York accent, his neat but informal appearance and welcoming air charmed us and made our children feel at home. At ages four and ten, our sons were physically active and highly inquisitive, but that did not bother Malamud. "What would you like to drink? Would root beer or ginger ale be all right? How about food? Maybe some cookies?" he asked. "I'll be right back," he assured us as he headed for the kitchen. Upon his return, he invited the boys to snack and then explore his home and grounds.

To my protests, he said, "let them have fun. What harm can they do? Don't worry about the rug and vases. They're just objects." Fortunately, however, the boys chose to romp outside on the spacious back lawn while we watched from the porch. Since Malamud disliked tape recorders, we chatted informally, with Malamud reminding us that his fiction was only loosely autobiographical. Although *A New Life* for example, was set in an Oregon College where he had taught for years, the "characters and events" were original. While the novel satirized provincial campus life, Malamud reassured me that he had actually enjoyed the place and still had friends there. He chuckled, remembering how a local newspaper had attacked him for defaming the community.

Deftly, Malamud shifted the subject from his work to mine. The
_____
[5]Avery family visit with Malamud, Bennington, VT, 10 July 1977.

interviewee was being interviewed. "How is your teaching? Are you able to teach and write?" he asked. "A twelve-hour load?" he exclaimed, "And two children to raise." "I certainly cannot complain about my schedule. I have been at Bennington College for sixteen years and really enjoy it. And why not?" he smiled. "I teach one course of my choosing for part of the year. The students are quite good, equal to some I taught at Harvard and Radcliffe. Only recently have I taught my own works in the seminar and the response has been gratifying. Teaching certainly is a two-way process in which I also learn." Pausing reflectively, he added, "there is so much to do. I helped to organize a writers' conference and as a result the college will have a M.F.A. program. We have invited distinguished authors. Tillie Olsen, for example, came and stayed with us for a few days." To my query about her personality and her work, Malamud responded carefully. "Her work, primarily, *Tell Me a Riddle,* is superb. She must really write more. As for her personality, she is a strong individual who makes demands and can be fussy."

When I asked whether he thought of her as a Jewish writer, he hesitated. "I am reluctant to label anyone," he replied. "People often praise *The Assistant* and *The Magic Barrel,* but they cannot be easily pigeonholed and I have written other works." While I agreed, I also pointed out that he could have fled his background and like Norman Mailer avoided the subject altogether. Smiling wanly, he replied, "I do not have Mr. Mailer's temperament. The critics should see beyond the window dressing. Even if the characters happen to be Jewish, they are human beings and what happens to them should matter to others. Critics should stop generalizing. Life is not that simple."

Before we left in the late afternoon, Malamud shook hands with our children. Looking seriously into the eyes of Peter, our ten-year-old, he said, "I like the way you handle life." To Daniel, our four-year-old, he said, "your mother made the right decision five years ago,"[6] an allusion to his remark to my thesis adviser in Oregon. With these few words, Malamud charmed us all and we left thankful for the time we had spent together.

Five years later, in the summer of 1982, I visited Bennington again. This time, he looked tired and pale, suffering from the after-effects of a stroke which left one arm weakened and his speech slightly slurred,

[6]Remark made at Bartel dinner reception, Eugene, OR, 3 August 1972.

a condition of which he was aware, although he ignored it once we began talking. Since I was participating in an NEH Seminar nearby in Massachusetts, Malamud had invited me to lunch with him and his wife, Ann, who prepared a simple but delicious meal. Although he did not help out, Malamud clearly appreciated his wife's efforts and she was pleased with his compliments.

Over lunch they talked about Bennington, which they considered their home along with New York where they resided for half the year. Malamud loved the contrast between the two settings, "the seasons, pace, the scenery; it's like having the best of both worlds," he remarked. We chatted about his work and he expressed relief that he had managed to finish his novel, God's Grace, despite his illness. "It's at the publishers now and should be available," he added, "within several months." "The title intrigues me. What is it about?" I asked. "I'd rather not say. Wait until it appears and we will talk about it. Though," he paused, "I don't think you will like it. It is not in the pattern of my other works. God's Grace is different, a departure for me and a real challenge."[7]

I was to recall his words months later when I reviewed God's Grace for the Jewish Monthly. Although impressed with the style, with his magical command for language, the subject and characters did not appeal to me. Within weeks of my lukewarm reaction, Malamud sent me a friendly note and a copy of Anthony Burgess' positive review, his polite way of setting me straight. I needn't have worried, however, about jeopardizing our friendship. Two years later when he appeared at Baltimore Hebrew University to receive an award for distinguished Jewish writing, Malamud seemed pleased that I would host him and Ann.

That November weekend was the last time I saw him. Though physically weak, Malamud was in top form. At the dinner reception, he good-naturedly autographed his books and answered repetitious questions. I was impressed by his modesty and reluctance to complain. Only once did a sour note surface when an elderly gentleman praised Saul Bellow's productivity. "Why, he's over seventy and still writing," the man exclaimed. "That's not difficult to do," Malamud interjected, "when you have your health, when you have been

[7]Bernard Malamud to Evelyn Avery, Bennington, VT, 13 July 1982.

blessed with a sound mind and body."[8] Yet despite his health, Malamud performed like a trouper, dramatizing portions of his work in progress, "The People," to the packed Baltimore Hebrew University audience. As his voice rose and fell, reflecting different characters, and an occasional chuckle escaped, it was evident that the author was enjoying himself. It was also clear that "The People," consisting of only sixteen unrevised chapters, reflects old patterns and new directions.[9]

By transforming a Russian Jewish peddler into an American Indian chief, Malamud reverses the process by which a Christian character such as Frank Alpine [*The Assistant*] identifies as a Jew. When the protagonist, Yozip Bloom, asks "What can I do for my people?" he is concerned about Indians, not Jews, from whom he feels alienated. In fact Yozip realizes that "the [Indian] cause . . . [provided] what he had lacked in his former, lonely life." Why should this "shtetl" loner fall in love with Native Americans? Why should this immigrant commit himself to tribal life? Perhaps, suggests Malamud, Indian life appeals to Yozip as a member of the lost tribe of Jewish Americans searching for their identity in the new world, a quintessentially American quest.

"The reader must feel free to choose," Malamud had once said about interpretations of his work. That evening the Baltimore Jewish audience embraced the author as one of their own. From his early works, Bernard Malamud had resisted the ethnic label, but like Yozip, he had been adopted to represent a tribe of wanderers, the tribe of American Jews.

[8]Bernard Malamud at Baltimore Hebrew University Dinner reception, November 1985.
[9]*The People and Other Stories* was published posthumously in 1989 by Farrar, Straus, and Giroux.

Index